multiple
intelligences

AND STUDENT ACHIEVEMENT:

SUCCESS STORIES FROM SIX SCHOOLS

LINDA CAMPBELL
and
BRUCE CAMPBELL

ASCD

Association for Supervision and Curriculum Development
Alexandria, Virginia USA

Association for Supervision and Curriculum Development
1703 N. Beauregard St. • Alexandria, VA 22311-1714 USA
Telephone: 1-800-933-2723 or 703-578-9600 • Fax: 703-575-5400
Web site: http://www.ascd.org • E-mail: member@ascd.org

Gene R. Carter, *Executive Director*
Michelle Terry, *Associate Executive Director, Program Development*
Nancy Modrak, *Director, Publishing*
John O'Neil, *Director of Acquisitions*
Mark Goldberg, *Development Editor*
Julie Houtz, *Managing Editor of Books*
Jo Ann Irick Jones, *Senior Associate Editor*
Gary Bloom, *Director, Design and Production Services*
Georgia McDonald, *Senior Designer*
Tracey A. Smith, *Production Manager*
Dina Murray, *Production Coordinator*
John Franklin, *Production Coordinator*
Kimberly Lau, *Desktop Publisher*
Hilary Cumberton, M.L. Coughlin Editorial Services, *Indexer*

Printed in the United States of America.

November 1999 member book (pc). ASCD Premium, Comprehensive, and Regular members periodically receive ASCD books as part of their membership benefits. No. FY00-2.

ASCD Stock No.: 199274
ASCD member price: $12.95   nonmember price: $15.95

Library of Congress Cataloging-in-Publication Data
Campbell, Linda
    Multiple intelligences and student achievement : success stories from
six schools / Linda Campbell and Bruce Campbell.
       p. cm.
"ASCD stock no.: 199274."
Includes bibliographical references and index.
    ISBN 0-87120-360-X (pbk. : alk. paper)
   1. Multiple intelligences. 2. Academic achievement. 3. Teaching. I.
Campbell, Bruce. II. Title.
    LB1060 .C364 1999
    370.15'2—dc21

                                         99-006910

04 03 02 01 00 99   10 9 8 7 6 5 4 3 2 1

MULTIPLE INTELLIGENCES AND STUDENT ACHIEVEMENT

SUCCESS STORIES FROM SIX SCHOOLS

ACKNOWLEDGMENTS

We thank John O'Neil at ASCD for his suggestion that we write this book and Howard Gardner for his challenge to demonstrate that MI can enhance student learning. We appreciate the insights and time graciously offered by the teachers, administrators, staff, parents, and students of EXPO for Excellence Elementary Magnet School, Key Learning Community, Lincoln High School, Mountlake Terrace High School, Russell Elementary School, and Skyview Junior High School as they helped us understand their beliefs, programs, and dynamic teaching and learning opportunities. We also thank Mark Goldberg at ASCD for his thoughtful editorial advice and his words of encouragement to "keep writing," and Jo Ann Jones at ASCD for her careful wordsmithing as the book took its final form. We appreciate the readers of this book for their interest in educational innovations that improve student achievement and that develop the multifaceted potential that resides within us all.

INTRODUCTION

Interest in Howard Gardner's theory of multiple intelligences and its application to education has been substantial since the publication of *Frames of Mind* in 1983 and Gardner's keynote address in early 1984, for a standing-room-only crowd at the Education Explosion Conference in Tarrytown, New York. More than a decade later, the attention focused on multiple intelligences (MI) remains unabated. Teachers, schools, and districts have embraced this model of intelligence as their guide amid much recent educational turmoil.

To date, however, the literature on MI theory in K–12 schools has been limited to how-to pedagogical applications or pilot classroom or school programs. *Multiple Intelligences and Student Achievement: Success Stories from Six Schools* is the first book to examine educational programs that have used MI for five or more years. It begins to answer questions that all educational innovations must ultimately address, such as, "How have MI programs affected student achievement?" and "Where and how were those results achieved?"

In search of answers to these questions, we contacted six public schools that claimed to have implemented MI programs for five or more years. The six schools—two elementary, two middle-level, and two high schools—serve a variety of student populations across the United States. Although each school's program is distinct, the programs resemble one another in two significant ways: MI provides a philosophic and curricular framework in each site, and the students have made significant academic achievement gains as measured by respected standardized tests, state assessment tests, and anecdotal comments from informed educators.

In writing the book, we wanted to understand the context and the processes of these MI-related successes. Chapter 1, "Why MI?", explores why a variety of teachers, grade levels, and disciplines have adopted Gardner's theory as an instructional framework. Our interviews with teachers at these sites revealed the powerful influence of teachers' beliefs on students and the effect of such beliefs on classroom learning.

Chapters 2, 3, and 4 each look at how teachers apply MI and examine student achievement gains. Each chapter describes two schools. Chapter 2 features Russell Elementary School in Lexington, Kentucky, and EXPO for Excellence in St. Paul, Minnesota. Chapter 3 surveys Skyview Junior High in Bothell, Washington, and the Key Learning Community in Indianapolis, Indiana. Chapter 4 reviews Mountlake Terrace High School in Mountlake Terrace, Washington, and Lincoln High School in Stockton, California. Because very little has appeared in the literature to date about implementing MI theory at the secondary level, we are especially pleased to include case studies of middle and high school programs.

To develop the six case studies, we interviewed teachers and administrators at each site; reviewed school documents (e.g., schedules, report cards, brochures, videotapes, and newsletters); conducted in-person observations of all schools; and gathered the following information from each program:

- Student and school demographics
- Who introduced MI to the school, as well as when and why
- Explanations of how the site became an MI program
- The nature of instruction and assessment before and after MI
- Changes in daily schedules, schoolwide curriculum, or other program components to accommodate MI
- Stories about MI's "official adoption" by the school staff
- Parent involvement and/or reactions
- Teachers' perceptions of students before and after MI
- Student achievement gains before and after MI.

After collecting data from teachers, administrators, students, and school documents, we analyzed and synthesized the information. The conclusions drawn reflect our views only, and we acknowledge the small sample size. In spite of these limitations, we anticipate that the experiences of these schools will have far-reaching implications for others. All six sites demonstrate that, one-by-one, schools change as much as those who work within them change. We used a consistent format for each school description to enable readers to quickly pinpoint information about a specific grade level or, if preferred, acquire a broader K–12 perspective of MI theory in action.

In the final chapter, "Lessons Learned from MI School Programs," we share information that these six schools have gained about transforming their environments, curriculum, assessment, student attitudes and achievement, and teachers' beliefs about those they teach.

We wrote *Multiple Intelligences and Student Achievement* for K–12 teachers, administrators, specialists, preservice educators, community members, and all others who believe that education is not only accountable for improving academic achievement but also for developing the multifaceted potential within each of us.

1 WHY MI?

" . . . You see, really and truly, apart from the things anyone can pick up (the dressing and the proper way of speaking, and so on) the difference between a lady and a flower girl is not how she behaves, but how she's treated. I shall always be a flower girl to Professor Higgins, because he always treats me as a flower girl, and always will; but I know I can be a lady to you, because you always treat me as a lady, and always will."

—Eliza Doolittle in *Pygmalion* by George Bernard Shaw

This quote from *Pygmalion* concludes Robert Rosenthal and Lenore Jacobson's book, *Pygmalion in the Classroom* (1968). As the character Eliza Doolittle explains above, a person's place in society is largely determined by how others treat her. Similarly, the famous Rosenthal/Jacobson study and ensuing book claim that students' intellectual development is influenced by teachers' expectations and beliefs about student ability.

In their original study, the Harvard researchers told teachers in a San Francisco elementary school that a new test had identified certain students as "bloomers," and that these children would make strong achievement gains during the school year. In reality, the identified students were selected at random without formal identification or testing. Yet, as the year progressed, the "bloomers," especially those in the early grades, did make significant achievement gains. Rosenthal and Jacobson attributed these gains to teachers' expectations and their differential treatment of identified students. The "Pygmalion effect," or the "self-fulfilling prophecy" states that what teachers expect from or believe about students influences how students perform.

Although controversy surrounded the original study, subsequent research has confirmed that teachers' beliefs do affect student outcomes (Bamburg, 1994; Brophy, 1983; Cooper & Tom, 1984; Good, 1987; Rist,

1970; Slavin, 1994; Winfield, 1986). Positive teacher expectations are recognized as a key variable that separates teachers who produce good achievement gains from those who do not. As a result, the educational mandate of maintaining high expectations for all students has become nearly cliché in school improvement efforts since the 1970s. What has not become cliché, however, is much specificity about the beliefs and behaviors that result in enhanced achievement. While teachers have always been entrusted with developing intellectual potential, the nature of such potential has seldom been discussed or described in educational circles, at least not until Howard Gardner proposed the theory of multiple intelligences.

TEACHER BELIEFS AND MI THEORY

Fifteen years after Harvard researchers Robert Rosenthal and Lenore Jacobson highlighted the connection between teacher expectations and student learning, another Harvard psychologist, Howard Gardner, suggested a model of intelligence that would rock the educational community as much as, if not more than, the "Pygmalion effect." While Rosenthal's research emphasized the importance of teacher beliefs about student intelligence, Gardner's work offered teachers a model of intelligence in which to believe.

The need for such a model was great. During preservice and inservice education, teachers rarely consider the nature of the human learning potential they are mandated to develop. This gap in our professional knowledge base is akin to doctors being trained without studying the human body or architects being licensed without understanding the physics that allow structures to remain upright. Subsequently, in faculty lounges, at workshops, and in the popular press, little teacher dialogue occurs about the extraordinary brain power of students. Many discussions frankly contradict such a notion! Although most teachers entered the field of education to improve the lives of others, achieving this aim is difficult without knowledge of the human intellect.

It was no wonder, then, that Gardner's theory of multiple intelligences immediately took root in the educational community. It offered a theoretical foundation of the mind and bolstered beliefs about student competence. Gardner was surprised by this ready adoption because he assumed his work would interest psychologists and intelligence scholars. In talking with educators, however, we have heard three reasons for their ready embrace of MI: (1) the theory's contribution to educators' knowledge base and beliefs about

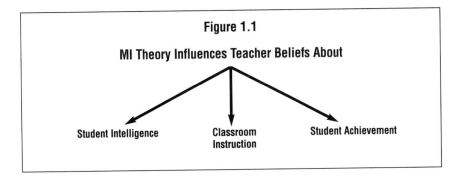

Figure 1.1

MI Theory Influences Teacher Beliefs About

Student Intelligence   Classroom Instruction   Student Achievement

the human mind, (2) MI's implications for professional practice, and (3) the impact of MI programs on student academic achievement. Among these three reasons, however, a single, compelling rationale emerged that explained the appeal of Gardner's work: *MI theory positively influences teacher beliefs*—beliefs about intelligence, instruction, and student achievement (see Figure 1.1).

MI THEORY AND TEACHER BELIEFS ABOUT INTELLIGENCE

Although theories about the nature of human intelligence have proliferated for centuries, such work has occurred in philosophic, psychological, and anthropological circles. Educators' preservice preparation typically does not delve deeply into such disciplines. When asked, "What is *intelligence?*" teachers are at a loss to define or describe it. The one theorist most teachers refer to when reflecting on intellectual development is the biologist-turned-psychologist Jean Piaget (1952). Piaget described aspects of cognitive growth, but his narrow view of human abilities and timetables has been shown to be inadequate. Laurie Nunnelee, an English teacher at Skyview Junior High School, claims, and others likely agree, that during preparation to become a teacher, "traditional IQ tests were mentioned, but they were our only exposure to the idea of intelligence." Teachers, for the most part, have lacked an adequate theory of human intelligence, yet they are responsible for the intellectual development of their students.

This shortcoming in professional training has exposed teachers and students to vulnerability in several ways. First, lack of formal education about human intelligence has left teachers to create their own theories of mind. As

Howard Gardner (1991) explains in *The Unschooled Mind,* both children and adults generate personal theories to explain their experiences and perceptions. The mind's theory-creating capacity seeks to extract meaning from and impose order upon life's innumerable experiences. Not based upon any existing knowledge, such theories emerge from an individual's best guesses at what seems plausible.

Teachers are not immune from theory generating. To make sense of the student learning potential they encounter daily, teachers construct beliefs or scripts about the intelligence of those in their charge. These implicit beliefs can be optimistic or pessimistic, constrictive or expansive. For the most part, they are seldom verbalized, usually unconscious, and may work against students' welfare. For example, if a teacher believes that intelligence cannot be modified, then schooling can accomplish little. Without educational intervention that might dislodge incorrect scripts about intelligence, or affirm and make conscious useful ones, teachers' implicit beliefs remain intact.

In our interviews with teachers and administrators, we encountered excitement about the theoretical foundation MI provides. MI offers insight into the human mind, its abilities, and its development that teachers find tangible, accessible, and professionally useful. The theory's helpfulness is evident in the comments of Edwina Smith, principal of Russell Elementary School: "As educators we say, 'All students can learn.' MI gives us something to back up that belief."

The theory is appealing in part because Gardner attributes specific functions to different regions of the brain. This neuroanatomical feature enhances the theory's credibility with teachers, other professionals, and lay populations. Teachers cite Gardner's work with a sense of confidence and security because it was generated by a foremost cognitive psychologist at one of the world's most prestigious institutions.

Further, Gardner's pragmatic definition of intelligence renders this usually murky construct manageable and concrete. In *Frames of Mind* Gardner (1983) describes intelligence as the ability to solve problems, to make culturally relevant contributions to one's community, and to identify new challenges to pursue. This definition focuses on dynamic processes—problem solving and contributing to others—common activities in most classrooms. Nor does the definition limit intelligence to a static, quantifiable number. Instead, it frees teachers from concerns of whether intelligence is genetically determined at birth to creating environments and instructional methods that develop all children's competencies. The definition emphasizes the cultural relativity of what is considered "intelligent behavior" and expands teachers' appreciation of diverse value systems and behaviors. As language arts teacher Chris Morgan at Lincoln High School says, "MI has made teachers more open and accepting of all students, which our growing minority population requires."

According to the theory of multiple intelligences, the mind's problem-solving capacities are multifaceted, exceeding the traditional view of intelligence as being verbally and mathematically bright. In 1983, Gardner identified seven forms of intelligence: linguistic, logical-mathematical, visual-spatial, bodily-kinesthetic, musical, interpersonal, and intrapersonal. A dozen years later, he added an eighth intelligence, that of the naturalist, one who specializes in recognizing and classifying natural and human-made phenomena. Recently, Gardner has suggested an additional intelligence: existential intelligence, which refers to the human desire to understand and pursue the ultimate questions, meanings, and mysteries of life. By making a case for many kinds of intelligences, Gardner affirms the observations of teachers who deal with a wide range of individual differences every day. For example, one student might play a musical instrument with ease but struggle with writing conventions. Another may enjoy the challenges of mathematical precision but avoid any opportunity to draw. Still another may perform a complex series of physical movements but appear awkward when interacting with peers.

Many teachers claim that MI provides a language or vocabulary to perceive and articulate a broader array of student talent. Teachers frequently express frustration with the limited forms of recognition available to students in traditional curriculums, where linguistic and mathematical skills dominate. With MI, educators can identify and affirm a wider spectrum of student competence. As John Moen, a multimedia teacher at Skyview Junior High School, explains, "For both teachers and students, MI creates a positive school culture of respect and belief."

TEACHER BELIEFS ABOUT INTELLIGENCE MADE EXPLICIT

The MI schools described in this book put structures into place for educators to make their beliefs about intelligence explicit. Typically, teachers formed study groups to read and discuss research on intelligence and engaged in professional development about Gardner's theory. In either approach, such discussions about the human mind were usually the first of their kind at the preservice or inservice level. As Pat Bolanos, principal of the

Key Learning Community, explains, "Howard Gardner's theory gave us a starting point for discussions about human intelligence, and to talk about why a student does well in one area but not in another."

The results of such discussions appear to have two different effects on teachers' beliefs about intelligence. According to Paul Osterlund, principal of EXPO Elementary School in St. Paul, "The theory has both affirmed and changed teachers' beliefs about intelligence." Many educators claim that MI makes their implicit beliefs about intelligence explicit. Some we interviewed stated they had always assumed students had diverse abilities. Laurie Nunnelee at Skyview Junior High explains, "I intuitively knew that students varied in their abilities and that all could improve. MI is reinforcing." Eeva Reeder, a math teacher at Mountlake Terrace High School, concurs: "MI affirmed what I intuitively knew about intelligence—that there are different ways to learn and process information. MI validates other meaning-making systems."

Some teachers, such as those at Key Learning Community, perceived MI as a theoretical ally because they wanted to educate the "whole child" and because they wanted to elevate the status of the arts in education. Others believed that all students should experience academic success and be acknowledged for their strengths. Social studies teacher Sherry Pratt at Lincoln High School claims that "with MI, teachers see students as more capable because they can demonstrate learning in a variety of ways. It gives students and teachers, all of us, chances to be acknowledged for our strengths. Confidence is boosted, and this encourages us to develop other areas too. MI adds a complexity and a richness to the classroom, and more experiences are honored in the classroom. It keeps me as a teacher more connected to the students."

While MI affirms many teachers' existing beliefs, other teachers find their beliefs challenged by the theory. Pat Bolanos, the principal of Key Learning Community, is adamant about the impact of MI on teachers' beliefs, "MI has absolutely changed teachers' basic notions of human intelligence." At Lincoln High School, teacher Chris Morgan explains that "MI has opened new horizons for the majority of our high school staff." Her colleague, chemistry teacher Pam Martin, agrees, "MI initiates a broader understanding of intellectual diversity."

Les Anderson, the founding principal of Russell Elementary School's MI program, provides a before and after description of the theory's influence on teachers' beliefs: "Teachers used to look at kids as having gaps in intelligence. Now they try to optimize learning power because they look for the positive instead of the negative. Teachers say things like, 'This child has trouble with reading, but he is good at art so we'll work from that strength.' And it works."

One primary teacher at Russell who resisted "the latest educational fad" was eventually won over by MI. Amy Littrell explains: "I was one of the most reluctant teachers in the school about adopting MI. Before I did, I'd find myself thinking at times, 'Some of these children are so low they can't do the work.' But then when I started using MI, I saw that they were really learning the material. They could do the work, and some became leaders."

Transformed beliefs of teachers sometimes extend beyond the classroom. Kathy Calwell, a middle school teacher at Key Learning Community, explains: "My perceptions of intelligence have changed significantly, first with students and then with everyone in the city—actually with people everywhere. I began to realize that every business and organization usually taps all intelligences."

In addition to affirming and, in some cases, changing teachers' beliefs, Gardner's theory has made another important contribution to education. MI provides a common language for articulating beliefs about students and instruction. According to Sandy Godbey, a primary teacher at Russell Elementary School, "The theory has immensely improved the quality of discourse with everyone at the school and also with the parents and community." Sandy's new principal, Edwina Smith, adds, "The teachers have a vocabulary that is different from what I was used to. They talk about how to help kids through their strengths. I haven't heard similar conversations at other schools."

MI THEORY AND TEACHER BELIEFS ABOUT INSTRUCTION

Understanding intelligence is a prerequisite to significant improvement in pedagogy. Adhering to the traditional notion of intelligence, schools identify certain skills as basic or essential, and they demean others by labeling them as frills. Narrowly defined limits of intelligent behavior make students who don't excel in linguistic or mathematical disciplines perceive their talents to be of little use. As Steven J. Gould states in *The Mismeasure of Man*: "We pass through this world but once. Few tragedies can be more extensive than the stunting of life, few injustices deeper than the denial of an opportunity to strive or even to hope, by a limit imposed from without, but falsely identified as lying within" (1981, pp. 28–29). MI identifies and dignifies many uses of the mind and, in so doing, suggests enriched educational opportunities for all students. At the same time, the theory does not dictate any single curricular approach. This lack of specificity appears to be a core reason for MI's adoption by the schools cited in this book. John Moen, at Skyview Junior High School, says that "MI runs counter to the societal trend to try to find the one best way to do something. MI opens things up and gives educators options."

There is no single, correct way to implement MI. Without a prepackaged program, or what principals Paul Osterlund and Edwina Smith call a "cookie-cutter" program, educators design curriculum as appropriate for their students. How they structure curriculum reveals their beliefs about how to enhance student learning. Some teachers offer numerous entry points into lesson content. Some, such as those at EXPO Elementary School, transform curriculums through arts-based instruction, multi-age classes, team-teaching, or interdisciplinary programs. Others, including teachers at Lincoln High School, emphasize self-directed learning through classroom projects, and still others at Key Learning Community and Skyview Junior High School deepen student expertise through apprenticeships. Unlike other educational reforms, MI is open to curricular interpretation.

When teachers adopt an MI approach to instruction, they confront unavoidable demands. Time is needed to develop multimodal lessons; to work as team members; to incorporate the specialties of librarians, PE, art, or music teachers; and to educate parents. Dan Wilson, a biology teacher at Mountlake Terrace High School, says, "MI lesson planning absolutely takes more time than other kinds. You can't just walk in and wing it. You have to be well prepared."

Anne McNeill, a primary teacher at EXPO for Excellence Elementary School, explains how, over time, MI instruction has become easier:

> One thing that has changed for me is I have realized that I don't have to teach everything well. I can get help from my colleagues. Gym, dance, and music teachers integrate the MIs into reading. They'll add movement and sign language and do poetry with music. That helps the rest of us a lot. There are a lot of built-in resources and modeling. Also, I let the kids show me ways they can learn. I provide ideas at the beginning, but then, as the year goes on, the students create their own performance assessments.

There are other benefits as well. As Lincoln High School Co-Principal Norrie Bean says, "With MI, teachers become the facilitators of learning. That makes their lives easier."

In most cases, teachers willingly make the extra effort because they would rather respond to student strengths than react to student deficits. High school math teacher Eeva Reeder explains that teaching through MI "creates a lot more work for me, but I am morally obligated to act on my understanding of human intelligence."

With higher expectations, with an emphasis upon strengths, teachers enrich their instruction and, in so doing, midwife improved student achievement. A high school student who had experienced academic failure before attending Lincoln's MI program said: "I am one of those interpersonal people. Older kids helped me here, and later I was able to help younger kids. Even though I am dyslexic, I could do my 'writing' sometimes on tape with outlines and visuals and still get credit. There is a lot more adaptivity here for my way of learning."

In the process, teachers undergo change themselves. Some enjoy renewed opportunities for intellectual and scholarly pursuits available in MI study sessions at the outset of their curricular changes. Nearly all the teachers we interviewed claim that teaching multimodally develops their creativity. At Russell Elementary School some intentionally develop areas of weakness, for example, by taking violin lessons with their students. Some, such as middle school teachers at Key, have taken professional leaps by teaching at universities or running summer programs for educators from the United States and abroad. With MI, teachers are shifting their focus and effort: from that of curriculum development to human development, including their own ongoing growth.

Regardless of how teachers interpret Gardner's theory, MI offers guidance for improving learning. The theory describes human intelligence while also suggesting the attributes of a well-educated person. With the dizzying complexities of teaching any group of students, there is great appeal in Gardner's model because it reveals both the source and the goal of intellectual development.

MI THEORY AND TEACHER BELIEFS ABOUT STUDENT ACHIEVEMENT

Teaching practices and classroom behaviors emerge from the beliefs educators have about their students. Sensitive to these perceptions, students respond to the unspoken attitudes of their teachers. For better or worse, student achievement mirrors the expectations of those who teach them. Simply put, teachers get from students what they expect.

Too often, teachers develop low expectations for students because of a number of limiting beliefs. Beliefs can be based on superficial factors, such as sex role stereotyping or negative assumptions about minority students, limited-English-proficiency students, those in poverty, those who turn in messy assignments, or wear unusual clothing, or sit in the back of the room. Gardner's theory of multiple intelligences corrects negative, implicit beliefs or inappropriate external factors that diminish expectations and weaken student achievement.

When asked how many special-needs children she had in her inclusive classroom, Arlene Desombre, a primary teacher at EXPO for Excellence, explained, "I don't see things that way anymore. I perceive children according to what they are good at rather than by their challenges." MI provides a new lens to perceive students and a new tool for acting on that information. One nearly unanimous assertion we encountered from our interviews is that when schools adopt MI, teachers intentionally seek strengths in every student. Katrina Wentzel, EXPO Elementary School's curriculum coordinator, "sees every child as gifted." Katrina's principal, Paul Osterlund, agrees: "MI has changed teachers' perceptions of our students. Everything is more personalized. They now teach children instead of books."

Because students are not perceived as defective, they have no excuses for not achieving well. High school biology teacher Dan Wilson emphasizes this point: "MI provides a vehicle to reach every kid. At the same time, we have higher expectations for students. We expect them to find ways to represent their knowledge with high-quality work. Students are more involved in their assignments." Principal Pat Bolanos further explains: "Our teachers have high expectations in all areas of intelligence. We have teacher specialists teaching in every area, and that raises the bar."

In addition to increased expectations for students, similar high expectations exist for the teachers themselves. Edwina Smith, principal of Russell Elementary School, says, "The teachers feel that more is expected of them with MI." Because problems of poor achievement do not lie in those they teach, educators must identify alternative approaches to tap the potential of their students. At many MI schools, educators attempt to personalize learning for each child. At EXPO for Excellence Elementary in St. Paul, former parent liaison Nancy Dana says: "MI has given us the motivation to look at each student as an individual. We believe that we all learn in different ways and that traditional educational approaches won't work for every child. We value differences in student ability."

With the belief firmly in place that all students possess strengths, student talents can be used strategically. For example, when students struggle with a concept or skill, they can often jump-start their learning by accessing their strengths, as numerous examples throughout the schools' case studies show.

We maintain that at schools where beliefs about intelligence remain implicit and limited, both students and teachers are at risk of underestimating and devaluing multiple forms of human talent. This situation contrasts markedly with what occurs at MI programs. Significantly, at MI schools, teachers' beliefs in students' abilities are communicated directly to the students themselves. Students come to perceive themselves as talented, sometimes in unexpected areas. A Key Learning Community middle school student says, "MI makes you learn different things about yourself. It brings out hidden talents." As a result of this positive self-regard, Principal Paul Osterlund says, "MI not only makes a positive difference in educational programs, it improves the lives of children."

When reflecting on an MI hypothesis that each person has a unique cognitive profile, teachers and students realize that MI pluralizes the concept of intelligence and of being academically challenged. Few people excel in all eight intelligences. Because everyone is talented in some areas and weak in others, students experience greater self-acceptance. All have much to learn and many areas in which to grow.

Aware that classrooms have long-lasting effects, teachers desire to help all students experience success. MI teachers, however, go beyond recognizing student talent. They provide concrete opportunities to develop their students' intellectual potential. With numerous skills in place, students are likely to experience success in multiple forms as they grow older.

Students in MI schools have high hopes and expectations for themselves. And why not? When an entire community of children, parents, and teachers believe that everyone is multi-talented, new forms of intellectual performance are likely. Student achievement gains increase as measured by standardized, state-mandated, and/or informal tests. While strong academic achievement cannot be attributed to a single factor, we maintain that teacher beliefs in MI significantly influence students to create positive self-fulfilling prophecies.

ELEMENTARY SCHOOLS, MI, AND STUDENT ACHIEVEMENT 2

"Disparity between black and white students' achievement has been eliminated. This is all the more remarkable because 94 percent of the school's population qualifies for free and reduced lunch."

—Les Anderson, former principal
Russell Elementary School, Lexington, Kentucky

"There are no longer the 'haves' and the 'have-nots' in our classrooms."

—Nancy Dana, former parent liaison
EXPO for Excellence Elementary Magnet School, St. Paul, Minnesota

Imagine what it would feel like to be labeled "multi-talented" from the first day you begin school. The students at Russell Elementary School in Lexington, Kentucky, and at EXPO Elementary in St. Paul, Minnesota, blossom with such regard and live up to their shared label. Russell Elementary evolved into an MI site as a natural extension of its curricular efforts. By contrast, EXPO for Excellence was founded as an MI program in 1990 and has remained one ever since. It is fair to say that just a few years ago neither of these schools gave a thought to achieving national visibility. Now, with their MI programs and resultant student academic success, their low profiles have been left behind, and educators are eager to visit these schools. Figure 2.1 provides a snapshot of the two elementary schools featured in this chapter.

Figure 2.1

A Snapshot of Two MI Elementary Schools

SCHOOL, LOCATION, DATE MI ADOPTED	STUDENT DEMOGRAPHICS	INSTRUCTION BEFORE MI	INSTRUCTION WITH MI	ASSESSMENT BEFORE MI	ASSESSMENT WITH MI	UNIQUE MI FEATURES
Russell Elementary School Lexington, Kentucky Adopted MI 1991–92.	Inner-city school of 195 students. Sixty-five percent are minority, and 94 percent are on free and reduced lunch.	Teacher-directed, mostly verbal, instruction.	Student-driven curriculum. Arts integrated into daily lessons in all classrooms. MI exploratory classes offered.	Written classroom tests. In 1992, on Kentucky state tests, students scored at 30th percentile with over 50 percent at the "novice" level.	Written classroom tests, projects, performances, and teacher observations. On state tests, scores doubled between 1992–96, without one student at the "novice" level.	All students take piano lab. Primary students write and perform an opera annually. Intermediate students pursue "MI majors."
Exposition (EXPO) for Excellence Elementary Magnet School St Paul, Minnesota Founded as an MI school in 1990.	Inner-city school of 720 students. Fifty percent minority, 50 percent on free and reduced lunch, and 35 percent ESL students.	MI since inception with thematic, in-depth MI curriculum, projects, and presentations.	Students learn content through MI in "family groups" that stay together for three years. Students select three MI "theaters" or electives per year based on their interests.	MI since its inception. Classroom assessments include multimedia work samples. Uses Metropolitan Achievement Tests.	Classroom assessments include multimedia work samples. On Metropolitan Achievement Tests, students at school three or more years score at 75th percentile.	All students work with MI specialists weekly. Three MI "theaters of learning" (electives) per year based on student choice.

Russell Elementary School in Lexington, Kentucky

School Demographics

Russell Elementary School is located near a busy intersection in inner-city Lexington, Kentucky. Built in 1954, the school has been used as a junior high and a senior high school. Although housed in an older facility, the school has been brightened by student murals. Russell's preschool through 5th grade program serves 195 students, 35 percent of whom are white and 65 percent are African American. Ninety-four percent of Russell's students qualify for free or reduced lunch, and 60 percent move within any given year. Ten regular classroom teachers each serve approximately 20 students. The grade-level divisions are fairly equal with four multi-age K–1 classrooms, three multi-age grades 2–3 classrooms, and three combined grades 4–5 classrooms. The school also employs full-time specialists in art, music, dance, media, and computer; three Title I staff members; and several instructional aides.

Why MI?

Initially, Russell Elementary School adopted MI for a single reason: to improve student achievement. During the 1980s, Russell students scored significantly below their district and county peers on standardized tests. This situation was expected to worsen with the newly mandated Kentucky Education Reform Act (KERA) of 1990 and its accompanying performance-based tests. Significant changes were needed to jump-start student achievement.

Important changes were occurring within the school. In 1991, Russell Elementary became the first school in the Fayette County Public School system to select a principal through a school-based decision-making process. Les Anderson was the principal ultimately chosen.

Creating an MI Program

Once on board for the 1991–92 school year, Anderson quickly appraised schoolwide instruction. The staff, for the most part, were veteran educators who relied on conventional teaching methods. Because such instruction was not yielding acceptable achievement gains, the staff was willing to consider alternative approaches. They were also concerned about the school's performance on the new state tests. MI was explored and later adopted as the foundation of the school's philosophy and program. Since the 1991–92

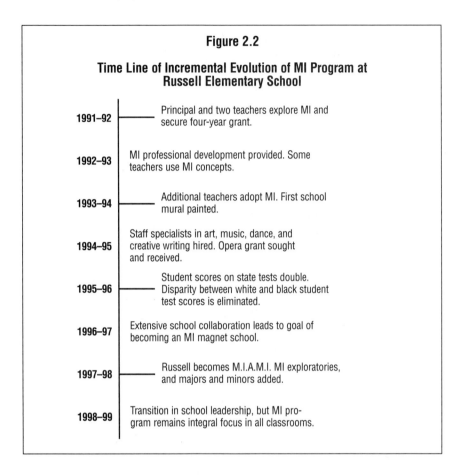

Figure 2.2

Time Line of Incremental Evolution of MI Program at Russell Elementary School

1991–92	Principal and two teachers explore MI and secure four-year grant.
1992–93	MI professional development provided. Some teachers use MI concepts.
1993–94	Additional teachers adopt MI. First school mural painted.
1994–95	Staff specialists in art, music, dance, and creative writing hired. Opera grant sought and received.
1995–96	Student scores on state tests double. Disparity between white and black student test scores is eliminated.
1996–97	Extensive school collaboration leads to goal of becoming an MI magnet school.
1997–98	Russell becomes M.I.A.M.I. MI exploratories, and majors and minors added.
1998–99	Transition in school leadership, but MI program remains integral focus in all classrooms.

school year, the MI emphasis at Russell evolved incrementally, as summarized in the time line in Figure 2.2.

1991–92: Anderson and two Russell teachers attended a conference and discovered MI. They were intrigued with integrating the arts into the classroom. To share their excitement with other staff members and to move the arts idea forward, Anderson provided two MI professional development opportunities for his teachers. He invited an MI consultant to the school who, as a classroom teacher himself, had improved standardized test scores with MI-based instruction. Anderson also sent three interested staff members to visit the Key School in Indianapolis, the nation's first MI model. The workshop and the school visit sparked schoolwide discussion about arts-based teaching and gave some staff members the rationale to radically alter their instruction. With emerging interest in MI, Russell applied for and received a four-year grant from the Kentucky Arts Council. The grant proposed integrating the arts into the classroom with MI as the philosophic and instructional vehicle.

1992–93: The arts grant made extensive staff development possible. Primary teachers began integrating the arts into their instruction and established MI learning centers in their classrooms. Similar to MI teachers elsewhere, these educators observed academic achievement increase and behavior problems decrease. The next step in MI adoption was to encourage other Russell teachers to diversify their instruction. Hesitant colleagues, especially at the upper elementary level, questioned the theory's usefulness with more complex content instruction.

1993–94: As part of the school's growing arts emphasis, students designed and painted the first large mural on a hallway wall. This activity launched Russell's annual mural painting tradition.

Also this year, the new state tests would hold each school accountable for student achievement. The tests were open-ended and performance-based in nature, and, as a result, more Russell teachers were nudged into piloting diverse instructional methods. They were immediately gratified by the increased enthusiasm and achievement of their students, even those who struggled the most. The success of the children most in need of success won over additional Russell staff members.

1994–95: Encouraged by student engagement, additional professional development, and ongoing grant funding, the Russell staff dedicated more of its daily schedule to MI. To do so, they employed specialists in art, music, dance, and creative writing. Further, as music echoed throughout the hallways, some teachers imagined creating a school musical. They wrote to the Metropolitan Opera and received a grant for the production of schoolwide operas. Beginning in 1995, Russell students began producing an original opera annually.

During this year, the school targeted improving its discipline program. The teachers' efforts to explicitly teach interpersonal and intrapersonal skills evolved into a schoolwide program called "Respect and Responsibility," which established a positive, safe, and respectful learning environment. Students generated and memorized school rules. They also identified the consequences for breaking them, as well as acknowledging good behavior.

Also during the year, former primary students made demands of some of their upper elementary teachers. Previously, they had learned through active, MI-based ways. In 4th and 5th grades, they wanted similar opportunities. In some cases, students took the lead in teaching their teachers about ways to learn with MI. For example, one 4th grader asked her teacher if she could compose a song for her classmates about an upcoming topic. With the teacher's permission, the girl taught her peers a content-based song she had written. Later, after testing them, the teacher discovered that all students not only passed but that many excelled on the material. From then on, she began diversifying her instruction.

1995–96: Student test scores doubled. Disparity between white and black student test scores was eliminated. When asked to explain the achievement gains, the principal has a ready response: "It's because of MI and nothing else!" Behavior improved dramatically throughout the school. Students suggested and then established a student council. Teachers identified star students of the month and, by students' request, also nominated star teachers of the month.

1996–97: New primary and intermediate teacher teams were formed that included every staff member. MI teaching took place in all classrooms. This year, even more of Russell's curriculum was dedicated to the multiple intelligences. All students began taking piano lab. With extensive school-wide collaboration in place, the teachers discussed and applied to become an MI magnet school.

1997–98: Russell became a citywide magnet school and assumed a new name: M.I.A.M.I. or Magnet for Integrated Arts Through Multiple Intelligences at Russell Elementary School. The new mission statement read:

> We believe that all students can learn when given opportunities, encouragement, and the means to develop their uniqueness in an educational setting. The mission of Russell Elementary School is to develop innovative practices in order to celebrate diversity, to personalize education, to identify, and to build upon each student's strengths through the multiple intelligences.

In keeping with their mission, the school added other innovative practices. MI Exploratories, for example, are offered during the last 45 minutes of the day. Over a year's time, every child rotates through exploratories in all seven intelligences. As students discovered their MI strengths, they carried these interests into their regular classrooms. MI "majors" and "minors" were also added. The 4th and 5th graders selected a major in art, band, orchestra, dance, creative writing, or computer math. The majors, scheduled for 45 minutes three times a week, developed students' strengths in-depth. To explore additional interests, students also selected minors, which were offered twice weekly. The entire school schedule revolved around its MI offerings.

1998–99: This was a year of acknowledgment and transition. The school's opera addressed fire safety, and three Russell teachers subsequently won the National Fire Safety Teacher of the Year Award. At a national fire-fighters' convention, the students taught firefighters about MI through their opera.

The year was significant in another way for Russell Elementary: Principal Les Anderson retired. Edwina Smith—an arts advocate, a former classroom teacher, and a former assistant principal to Les Anderson—became the new principal. Even with the leadership change, the school's strong program continues as a citywide multiple intelligences magnet. Les Anderson works for the Lexington School District part-time and consults nationally on improving inner-city students' academic achievement through a multiple intelligences program.

THE MI CURRICULUM

Before the advent of MI, most teaching at Russell could be characterized as "traditional." Primary teacher Amy Littrell describes previous instructional approaches: "Before, it was all based on basals and teaching out of textbooks. Now we use these as resources. There was also more written assessment, but not more learning."

The evolution of Russell's MI program was incremental. Initially, two teachers and a principal were intrigued by Gardner's theory. As student achievement improved in these classrooms, other staff members took instructional risks. Now, all Russell teachers use MI as a framework for lesson planning. Over time, they have refined their MI instruction. As primary teacher Sandy Godbey explains, "At first, I would have to say we had a lot of 'fluff.' Each year we reevaluate, direct our curriculum and our MI efforts, and eliminate the fluff."

In addition to lesson planning, MI drives the entire school program. The individual intelligences, and especially the arts, claim significant amounts of the school's schedule. Also, instead of chronological grade levels, Russell students attend flexible, multi-age classes. As primary teacher Dana Messner explains, "Students work in groups and move from one classroom to another, depending on their needs in a given subject." The flexible groupings and arts emphasis are evident in the daily primary schedule shown in Figure 2.3.

The primary students spend part of each day at MI *learning centers,* named after well-known individuals who exemplify each intelligence. Students study how the experts developed and used their talents. In this way, highly gifted individuals become "mentors in absentia" for Russell

Figure 2.3

Sample Russell Elementary School Primary Schedule

7:30–7:45	Morning activities
7:45–8:15	Orchestra class
8:15–9:15	Flexible skill groups
9:15–10:15	One of the following: library, computer, music, or art
10:15–10:55	MI centers
10:55–11:45	Lunch
11:45–12:45	Flexible skill groups
12:45–1:00	Physical education
1:00–2:00	Flexible skill groups
2:00–2:10	Preparation for dismissal

—Reproduced with permission of Russell Elementary School.

students. The names of the centers rotate, but an example of their names for the 1998–99 school year included:

- Whitney Houston for musical intelligence
- Helen Keller for intrapersonal intelligence
- Malcolm X for interpersonal intelligence
- Dr. Seuss for linguistic intelligence
- George Washington Carver for logical-mathematical intelligence
- Shaquille O'Neal for kinesthetic intelligence
- Donatello for visual-spatial intelligence

Centers-based instruction is thematically organized. It is also based upon student interests. For example, one year, when a student at Russell was killed tragically in an apartment fire, her classmates wanted to learn how to prevent similar casualties. Because of their students' interest, the teachers used fire safety for an MI lesson. Their MI centers revolved around the academic expectation that students would demonstrate using fire safety and other life skills.

At their MI centers, students memorized and sang fire safety songs, read diaries of survivors of apartment building fires and role-played their experiences, wrote and performed a mock newscast about a city fire, identified school escape routes around the building, wrote directions for orderly fire drills at school, read and drew two escape routes for different home and apartment floor plans, and put together a paper model of a fire truck to learn its special features. It was this MI centers-based lesson that ultimately inspired the students' opera on fire safety.

In contrast to former years, the school opera is no longer a schoolwide event but rather an annual 2nd and 3rd grade project. Since its inception, the opera production has become steadily more student-driven. As former Principal Les Anderson explains:

> The students do all the work. They write and perform the script, do the lighting, send out press releases and invitations, and make the scenery. Recently, they constructed a set on wheels that turns around quickly to show another set on the other side. They are learning so many things that apply to real life, including the use of academic skills. One production manager, an 8-year-old, went from 1st grade, first month in his reading scores to 3rd grade, fifth month in half a year's time because of his motivation to do his job well.

The annual opera is produced by the Russell Elementary Small-People-Doing-Big-Deeds Opera Company. One example of a student-written script is the 1997 opera entitled "Responsibility in Deed." The storyline opens with a boy named Chuck who takes care of his sick father while his mother works long days to pay her husband's medical bills. Chuck cannot play after school because he is needed at home. Chuck's friends miss him and decide to help the family by raising extra money. The group plans and carries out a variety of odd jobs and, as the money comes in, one of Chuck's friends is spotted with a large stack of dollars rolled up in his hand. Not knowing about the group's project, a bystander assumes the boy has stolen the money and, thus, the plot quickly thickens.

Intermediate students engage in other MI activities. Fourth and 5th grade students pursue intelligence majors and minors of their choice. They are mentored by the school's certified specialists. As a brochure describing the school claims, each student at M.I.A.M.I. at Russell receives "a well-balanced education that will put you on top of the world."

Russell teachers take personal responsibility for teaching students through their strengths. Because of the school's shared belief that all students are talented, teachers look for student talent. Because MI identifies what to look for, teachers become better observers of their students and, as a result, are able to diversify instruction for each youngster. For example, one 7-year-old was not making adequate progress in reading. Her teacher was aware, however, that the girl excelled at drawing and that her sketches included complex and intricate details. Calling the girl's attention to her well-developed perceptual and fine motor abilities, the teacher helped her apply these same skills to word recognition and spelling. The student, while confronting a challenge, nevertheless kept her self-esteem in tact. She also learned the important lesson that her gifts could be used in multiple ways. Russell teachers are informed observers who personalize instruction so that students succeed. Figure 2.4 shows the cycle that leads to success.

Another instructional change inspired by MI is a shift from teacher-directed to student-directed learning. Teachers give students choices of how to learn and how to demonstrate their learning. In so doing, teachers have come to see students as capable and creative and have subsequently turned over additional responsibilities to them. For example, Russell students initiated and currently run their own conflict resolution program; mentor new

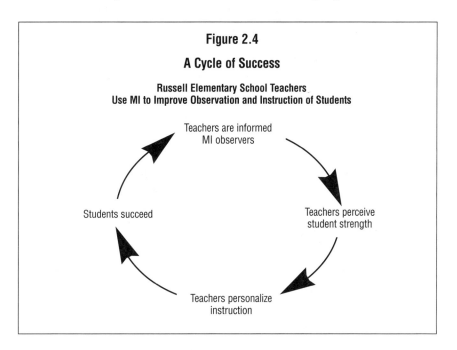

Figure 2.4

A Cycle of Success

**Russell Elementary School Teachers
Use MI to Improve Observation and Instruction of Students**

Teachers are informed
MI observers

Teachers perceive
student strength

Teachers personalize
instruction

Students succeed

classmates; design and write the school's brochures, folders, and character education handbooks; select a teacher of the month; and run a friendship club for peers who would benefit from "random acts of kindness."

DEVELOPING CHARACTER

In addition to the strong, arts-enriched academic curriculum, Russell explicitly addresses the personal intelligences. A schoolwide character education program identifies interpersonal and intrapersonal skills students must master. In the fall, Russell students receive Character Education Handbooks listing the skills that will be taught throughout the year. Each week, one new skill is discussed and applied. For example, at the outset of the 1998–99 school year, students practiced listening in all classes. This skill is described as follows in their Character Education Handbooks:

Skill 1: Listening
1. Look at the person who is talking.
2. Sit quietly.
3. Think about what is being said.
4. Respond to what is being said with a gesture or comment.
5. Ask a question about the topic to learn more.

Throughout the school year, additional skills are introduced and studied. A few examples are shown in Figure 2.5.

Russell's character education is an important component of the total school's discipline efforts, called the Respect and Responsibility Plan. Believing that students and staff have a right to a safe, secure, and respectful environment, Russell teaches its students to be responsible citizens. There

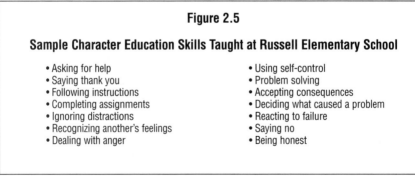

Figure 2.5

Sample Character Education Skills Taught at Russell Elementary School

- Asking for help
- Saying thank you
- Following instructions
- Completing assignments
- Ignoring distractions
- Recognizing another's feelings
- Dealing with anger

- Using self-control
- Problem solving
- Accepting consequences
- Deciding what caused a problem
- Reacting to failure
- Saying no
- Being honest

—Reproduced with permission of Russell Elementary School.

are tangible rewards for positive behavior. The students have creative learning opportunities.

Engaging Inner-City Parents

As is common with many inner-city schools, Russell Elementary has historically had little parental involvement. When the school was evolving into an MI site, few parents questioned its mission or efforts. A challenge facing Russell was not one of educating parents about MI's value, but rather of drawing their attention to what was happening at school in the first place. Principal Edwina Smith explains some of the difficulties in reaching out to parents:

> The majority of our parents do not see education as a high priority in their lives. Sixty percent of our 3rd graders do not finish the school year with us. Their parents are concerned with food and safety issues. In fact, I went to meet one parent whose child never came to school. The mother told me she had no electricity, heat, or any way to cook at home, and could not afford to buy clothes for her child to attend school. When I explained that we could feed and clothe her child, she cried. We are advocates rather than authoritarian figures for our families.

One way that Russell has engaged inner-city parents is by dedicating portions of PTA meetings to student performances. For example, students present creative writing selections, play the piano, and sing accappella at the meetings. Similarly, when parents attend the opera productions and see their children in action, they, just as the teachers, perceive talents in each student. Sometimes, parents see new possibilities for themselves.

One 3rd grade boy, after learning to read at school, began teaching his father how to read at home. When the student was in 5th grade, he taught his father cursive writing. Even though 94 percent of Russell's students receive free and reduced lunch, there is a growing sense of optimism and hope about what education can accomplish in this inner-city community.

Student Achievement

Russell's initial rationale for adopting MI was to improve student achievement. There was much work to be done. Students typically fared poorly on standardized measures, and, in 1990, the sweeping Kentucky Education Reform Act (KERA) mandated an additional performance-based test called the Kentucky Instructional Results Information System (KIRIS). Each school would be held accountable for its achievement results, and the testing approaches were dramatically different from traditional measures. On the KIRIS, test items include open-response questions and accountability portfolios in writing and math, and require the use of higher-order thinking skills. Students are assessed in seven disciplines and at four levels:

- *Novice:* The student is just beginning to understand new knowledge and skills.
- *Apprentice:* The student has gained some knowledge and skills.
- *Proficient:* The student understands main disciplinary concepts and can do nearly all tasks.
- *Distinguished:* The student demonstrates advanced skills and knowledge.

It was no surprise in 1992, the first year that KIRIS was administered, that Russell students scored at the 30th percentile with over 50 percent scoring at the novice level in basic skills. With their MI program more securely in place by 1993, the school surpassed its own improvement goals. Similar results occurred for the next three years.

These achievement gains are not attributable to the "halo effect," which occurs when a new program achieves temporarily improved results. At Russell, the test scores have steadily increased, so much so that, by 1996, student scores doubled from their baseline in 1992. During this school year, two other noteworthy test results were evident:

1. Not a single student scored at the novice level, a feat only 2 other elementary schools out of 35 in the county accomplished.

2. The discrepancy between black and white student scores disappeared.

In addition to the state-administered tests, Russell kindergarten students also take Metropolitan Readiness Tests. When the 1997–98 year began, Russell's goal was for all students to read at grade level by year's end. The 38 kindergarten students met the goal a month ahead of schedule, achieving similar results on the math portion of the test. In many cases, the students' spring 1998 scores had more than tripled their fall 1997 scores. Former Principal Les Anderson explains the academic gains: "Russell has such an enriched atmosphere, the children can't help but learn."

The school's academic success has attracted much attention. Russell has been acknowledged by its county as a "Pacesetter School" and by the state of Kentucky as a "Rewards School." It has been spotlighted in local and national media. It frequently hosts visitors, for example, researchers from Harvard and from the National Endowment for the Arts.

After spending time at the school, visitors typically agree that educational innovation, at least at Russell, does not mean ignoring the basics, but is about improving basic skill achievement and more. It also means transforming teachers' beliefs. At Russell, teachers demand much of their students. They forego dismissing any student as incapable, and they no longer attribute weak achievement to external influences. Instead of giving up on their students or feeling sorry for them, the teachers maintain unwavering high expectations. Children are susceptible to such influences. Russell students, emulating their teachers, expect to do well, and their self-fulfilling prophecies are realized.

EXPO FOR EXCELLENCE ELEMENTARY MAGNET SCHOOL IN ST. PAUL, MINNESOTA

SCHOOL DEMOGRAPHICS

EXPO for Excellence Elementary Magnet School is an inner-city K-6 school of 720 students in St. Paul, Minnesota, which was founded as an MI magnet school. Since its inception, the school has been located in the only available facility in the district, a former Catholic high school building. Although 50 percent of EXPO's students are on free and reduced lunch, the student body represents a range of socioeconomic diversity. Fifty percent of the students are minority. Another 35 percent are ESL students.

The school has 29 classrooms with full-time teachers; 10 teaching assistants; 4 educational assistants; and 19 full- and part-time specialists in special education, the visual arts, bodily-kinesthetics, music, and English-as-a-second-language. Student-to-teacher ratios vary. The all-day kindergarten classes have a 23 to 1 ratio. By state mandate, 1st grade classrooms have 18 students each. This number increases significantly in grades 2 and 3, where there is a 27 to 1 ratio. And in grades 4 through 6, there are 29 students to 1 teacher.

WHY MI?

EXPO Elementary was conceived of as an MI magnet school in the late 1980s by a small group of St. Paul school district administrators, teachers, and parents. They had two strong rationales for establishing an MI program. The first was to create a school based upon state-of-the-art research and theory. Contemporary studies of learning, development, and intelligence indicated ways to improve education for all students. Gardner was a leading cognitive sciences researcher, and the EXPO group hoped to demonstrate that cognitive theory in practice would yield enhanced student outcomes. The school's name, "Exposition (EXPO) for Excellence" Elementary Magnet School, reflected its commitment to applying cutting-edge research to teaching and learning.

Along with their desire to create a state-of-the-art cognitive sciences program, the EXPO group also wanted to transform gifted education. The district's traditional gifted and talented school, which tested for admissions, resulted in what some called intellectual elitism. EXPO founders maintained that an MI program would communicate the belief that every child was gifted. Citing Gardner's research on outstanding achievers in diverse fields, group members rejected the notion that traditionally identified gifted students had any monopoly on intellectual strengths. Instead, they hypothesized that giftedness could be developed through enriched learning experiences. If teachers perceived their students as gifted and proceeded accordingly, the "enormous potential of students," as EXPO's brochure cites, would be realized.

CREATING AN MI PROGRAM

In the late 1980s, a St. Paul school board member and a staff development administrator considered the possibility of creating an MI elementary school of choice. The timing seemed appropriate. Minnesota had extensive legislation promoting schools of choice, and the St. Paul School District already featured successful magnet programs. The administrators knew that if others supported their idea, an MI magnet school would likely result. After approaching other district personnel, the administrators quickly saw their original group grow in size to include supportive teachers, principals, and parents.

Although their enthusiasm was extensive, the group soon confronted the reality of limited district resources, including staff development, to inform their work. Undaunted, group members took it upon themselves to learn about MI. A founding administrator organized study sessions to read and discuss Gardner's work, review other MI programs, and envision what this new school might look like.

The philosophy and curriculum of the school quickly took form. The group determined that the EXPO model would begin as a K–3 school, with multi-age groupings and program components that actively developed each intelligence. The excitement of the founders fueled their perseverance through the unforeseen challenges ahead.

During 1988–89, the group wrote a grant and sought the district's formal approval for opening an MI magnet school in the fall of 1990. They were sorely disappointed when the grant proposal was rejected and a supportive administrator left St. Paul for another position. Although the district did approve the MI magnet school, at first staff could not locate a building. Without other options and amid much controversy, the St. Paul School District purchased a former parochial high school in May 1989. Some citizens in the Catholic community objected to the sale of their building, and many St. Paul teachers claimed it lacked amenities for young children. Nevertheless, the facility was purchased and renovated and the interior designed to accommodate MI learning opportunities. With the school building and program in place, all that was needed were students. The new program was advertised through district announcements, newspaper articles, and, most important, through word-of-mouth by interested parents.

EXPO for Excellence Elementary Magnet School opened in fall 1990 as a K–3 program with 310 students. Since then, the school has added a grade level each year to reach its current configuration as a K–6 elementary school of 720 students.

MI CURRICULAR FEATURES

During the 1997–98 year, EXPO students proudly wore T-shirts commemorating their school's short history: *EXPO celebrates seven years of the seven intelligences.* The students have many reasons to celebrate. Though much of the restructuring literature recommends personalizing education for students, EXPO accomplishes this goal. The entire curriculum emphasizes the personal intelligences. While many educational programs focus on "curriculum development," at EXPO the teachers are equally concerned with "human development."

SCHOOL AS FAMILY

At EXPO every child belongs to a learning family. The kindergarten family is named the Garden. The four primary families include the Apples, Evergreens, Ginkgos, and Redwoods, and the three intermediate families are named Banyan, Oak, and Willow. Each family group has approximately 100

students, and with the exception of kindergarten, the primary and intermediate families are multi-age. Students and teachers have three years to learn
about one another, personalize instruction, and benefit from the consisten-
cy and security of relationships developed over time.

In addition to the larger family groupings, students are assigned to
smaller "homebase" classrooms. At the primary level, children remain with
their homebase from 1st through 3rd grade. At the intermediate level, students join a new homebase and may again remain with a teacher and classmates for three years.

Special education students are easily accommodated with the school's
family groupings. Because homebase is the basic unit of EXPO, the Learner
Assistance Team of specialists support homebase teachers by co-planning
curriculum and carrying out individualized instruction, if required. This collaborative, integrated approach ensures that special-needs students spend a
significant portion of the day in regular education settings.

Teachers, students, and parents all appear to value the enduring relationships facilitated by the school's multi-year schedule. Teachers claim that
they have time to develop effective techniques for each student and that a

---

Figure 2.6

EXPO for Excellence Elementary Magnet School's LIFESKILLS

Caring:	Feeling concern for others
Common sense:	Using good judgment
Cooperation:	Working together for a common goal or purpose
Courage:	Acting according to one's beliefs
Curiosity:	A desire to learn or know about one's world
Effort:	Trying and working diligently
Flexibility:	The ability to alter plans when necessary
Friendship:	The skill of making and keeping friends through mutual trust and caring
Initiative:	Doing something because it needs to be done
Integrity:	Conducting oneself according to a sense of what is right and wrong
Organization:	Planning, arranging, and implementing in an orderly way; keeping things in an orderly, reusable fashion
Patience:	Waiting calmly for someone or something
Perseverance:	The ability to continue in spite of difficulties
Problem solving:	Seeking solutions to challenging problems or situations
Responsibility:	Responding when appropriate and being accountable for one's actions
Sense of humor:	The ability to laugh and be playful without hurting others

positive classroom culture perpetuates itself through the returning students. They also like team planning and team teaching, and sharing knowledge about students with colleagues in the same family grouping.

Students forge strong bonds with teachers and classmates. Similarly, parents come to view their children's school family as extended family, one with the common goals of promoting academic success and enjoying one another's company at school pizza parties and overnights. Because of the strong attachments that develop among students, teachers, and parents, EXPO has developed transition processes to accommodate the change in teachers and peer groups between the primary and intermediate years.

HEAD, HANDS, AND HEART: THE PERSONAL INTELLIGENCES

Some educators view the personal intelligences as nebulous, controversial, and unassessable. Some claim that social and emotional skills and values are family matters and not the purview of schools. EXPO, however, takes a stance similar to Howard Gardner, who asserts that the personal intelligences ultimately determine success in life. As a result, EXPO has created a Behavior Curriculum that explicitly teaches aspects of interpersonal and intrapersonal intelligences. This curriculum relies on part of Susan Kovalik's Integrated Thematic Instruction Model (1994). Kovalik identifies how students can attain their "Personal Best" through acquiring the LIFESKILLS shown in Figure 2.6.

From kindergarten onward, EXPO teachers and students discuss these qualities, role-play and model them, use them in goal-setting sessions, feature them as curricular themes, and assess them. EXPO's emphasis on the personal intelligences reinforces for students that more than good reading and clear writing are required to be accomplished adults. Positive attitudes, belief in one's abilities, and competent follow-through are also necessary.

INDIVIDUALIZED GOAL-SETTING CONFERENCES

Another way that EXPO emphasizes the personal intelligences is by targeting learning goals for each student at goal-setting conferences held twice yearly. The first is scheduled at the beginning of the school year. Before attending the conference, parents and their children are asked to reflect on student strengths, weaknesses, and interests, and to identify three or four yearlong goals. When the teacher, student, and parents meet, they discuss, fill out, and sign forms that specify student strengths and individual goals. Through this three-way conversation, EXPO students come to understand themselves as learners. The goal-setting conferences are organized with

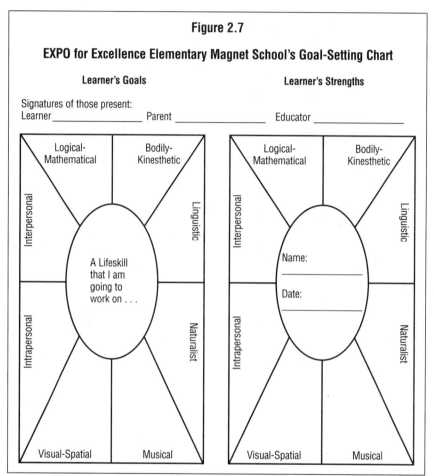

Figure 2.7

EXPO for Excellence Elementary Magnet School's Goal-Setting Chart

Learner's Goals   Learner's Strengths

Signatures of those present:
Learner_____ Parent _____ Educator _____

Logical-Mathematical   Bodily-Kinesthetic
Interpersonal   Linguistic
A Lifeskill that I am going to work on . . .
Intrapersonal   Naturalist
Visual-Spatial   Musical

Logical-Mathematical   Bodily-Kinesthetic
Interpersonal   Linguistic
Name:_____   Date:_____
Intrapersonal   Naturalist
Visual-Spatial   Musical

—Reproduced with permission of EXPO for Excellence Elementary Magnet School.

forms based upon the multiple intelligences. Figure 2.7 shows two of the forms used.

Throughout the school year, students are encouraged to pursue their goals in class and to gather work samples that demonstrate their growth. In early spring, during the second round of goal-setting conferences, student progress is reviewed, and their goals are revised and updated. At the end of the year, parents review student portfolios and see evidence of their children's gains in multiple areas. Primary teacher Arlene Desombre describes the portfolios as "celebrations of growth."

Although goal setting requires extra teacher time, the staff are committed to it because it teaches students that positive attitudes and behaviors result in accomplishment. They learn that meaningful work requires sustained and disciplined effort. Teachers also observe that students shoulder more responsibility for their learning and, in so doing, meet EXPO's schoolwide goal of creating self-directed learners.

THEMATIC MI CURRICULUM

At EXPO, the school "families" have much autonomy in the curriculum they pursue. With the exception of a math block that occurs at the same time daily, each family determines its daily schedule as well as the content of the curriculum. Without the imposition of a schoolwide master schedule, time is used as a resource. Schedules vary among family groups and are determined by the content to be taught. One constant is that MI theory is evident in each classroom environment, in all curriculum units and assessment measures, and in the vocabulary students and teachers use daily.

Curriculum at EXPO is thematically organized. Themes are selected from three sources: student interests, teacher goals, and the district's specified outcomes. Sample themes have included People, Patterns, and Power; Piece by Peace We Build Our Community; Cultures: The Meeting of Many Minds; and Inventions.

By teaching thematically, teachers infuse MI throughout units and emphasize the problem-solving and problem-finding aspects of Gardner's definition of intelligence. For example, when studying the intermediate-level theme "Inventions," students explored simple machines using Lego building kits, experimented with electricity and magnetism, wrote journal entries about their findings, read biographies of inventors, hypothesized about how small appliances work, took apart and put the machines together, and created their own inventions to solve problems they identified. In addition to learning through several intelligences, students investigated significant questions about how their world works.

EXPO teachers maintain that while instruction and the total school program is dedicated to the multiple intelligences, they remain focused on important content and skills, as the Invention unit reveals. As primary teacher Anne McNeill explains, "We ask ourselves, 'Why are we doing this?' We try to make sure that we focus on the real purpose in what we are teaching. Not every moment in the classroom has to be fun. It is more important that learning is purposeful and of value. I talk about this with the kids. The real job here is to teach and to show progress, not just be entertaining."

Another EXPO primary teacher, Kathlyn Michel, echoes this sentiment: "Kids really want to come to school everyday. They have positive attitudes because learning is fun and purposeful. They don't want to miss a minute. For example, one student had a dental appointment during the middle of the day and came back at the end just to be here for the last 20 minutes."

MI APPRENTICESHIPS

Gardner recommends that schools offer three apprenticeships to develop student talent: one in an art form, another in an academic area, and a third in a physical discipline. In apprenticeships, students should be mentored by experts possessing real-world skills and knowledge. By learning from adult role models, students can glimpse where their efforts might lead.

Without using the term, EXPO offers two forms of apprenticeships, one provided by building specialists and another through the school's "Theaters of Learning." While thematic instruction in the regular classrooms teaches *through* the intelligences, EXPO's apprenticeships develop individual student intelligence in-depth. Both activities share the common goal of nurturing a broad spectrum of student talent.

To challenge students in each discipline, EXPO's building specialists serve as "intelligence" experts. The specialists mentor rotating "family" groups in musical, kinesthetic, mathematical, and visual intelligences. Their programs span one to four weeks and often build upon homebase themes. The specialists offer in-depth instruction in areas that are minimized in many school curriculums. They teach students that all forms of expressive representation, whether visual, kinesthetic, or verbal, are valid and important, and should be done well.

The second form of mentoring occurs in EXPO's Theaters of Learning. "Theaters" are elective classes offered three times a year for eight weeks. To create small class sizes, all EXPO faculty and administrators teach a theater, all of which are open to any interested students in the school.

Theaters highlight the different intelligences. Through these electives, students are encouraged to pursue their passions or to risk developing a latent capacity. Together with their parents, students choose a different theater to attend during fall, winter, and spring terms. Making a selection can be a daunting task. Often, students can choose from as many as 30 options with titles like, "Abracadabra! The Science of Magic," "Animals in Nature and Art," "Kitchen Wizards," "Team Sports," "Sign Language Safari," and "Hmong Literacy," a topic to promote understanding of this southeastern Asian culture. If a student were to choose Puppet-Making as a theater to attend, he or

---

Figure 2.8

**MI Theater of Learning Form Used at
EXPO for Excellence Magnet Elementary School**

Theaters of Learning

Learner: _____   Educator: _____

Theater: ___Puppet-Making_____   Term: _____

Class Description: Do you like to color and paint, cut and glue, plan and design, imagine and create? In this theater, learners will explore puppetry through creating puppets of their own. We will experiment with finger puppets, stick puppets, felt puppets, and papier-mâché puppets.

Intelligence Focus: Visual/Spatial (designing), Musical/Rhythmic (poems and songs), Logical/Mathematical (creating and using patterns, measurement), Interpersonal (cooperation, group work).

Educator Comments: _____

_____

_____

_____

—*Reproduced with permission of EXPO for Excellence Elementary Magnet School.*

she would fill out the form shown in Figure 2.8, with a place for comments by the teacher.

EXPO apprenticeships move students beyond work sheets, textbooks, and questions posed by others. Students acquire the skills of artists, writers, photographers, and experience the thrill of gaining real-world knowledge, thinking for themselves, and being inventive and creative.

SMALL IS BEAUTIFUL BECAUSE OF LARGE SCHOOL OPPORTUNITIES

EXPO's curriculum is structured to address each student's interests, strengths, and needs. Such individualized attention is usually found in small classes available for honors or private school students. EXPO's model, however, goes beyond what many exclusive programs might offer. Because of its size and MI commitment, the school has a large staff whose teaching methodologies develop the multifaceted minds of its students in personalized ways. Through family groupings, students work in small, stable communities. With multi-age instruction, they are challenged to work at appropriate levels in many disciplines, regardless of their ages. With thematic teaching, students learn through the multiple intelligences. Through goal setting, students, parents, and teachers establish individualized learning plans that are reviewed and updated. Through working with specialists and theaters of learning, students are mentored in real-world skills by experts and develop a broader spectrum of their potential. EXPO's curriculum is an example of small is beautiful amid an elementary student population with over 700 students, which is still growing.

Figure 2.9

Teaching EXPO for Excellence Elementary Magnet School Parents About MI

From School to Home:

1. **MI Mind Maps:** Teachers send home mind maps of each thematic unit's content and MI activities.

2. **MI Homework:** Students take home MI assignments that siblings and parents may help complete and that they may help present in class. MI homework is given before every school break and is favorably anticipated by students and parents alike.

3. **Telephone Calls:** Teachers make impromptu calls home when students have performed especially well in challenging intelligence areas.

4. **Videotapes:** Classroom videotapes are sent home showing academic and personal intelligences achievement of individual students or small-group projects.

5. **Theaters of Learning:** Parents and students select three six-week apprenticeships in one or more intelligences.

From Home to School:

6. **Cabarets:** Once a year, family groupings present an evening cabaret to demonstrate what they have learned from the school's intelligence specialists.

7. **Goal-Setting Conferences:** Parents, teachers, and students meet at school twice yearly to identify, update, and review students' intelligence goals.

8. **Classroom Environments:** Each classroom has resources, centers, and/or displays featuring all eight intelligences. When parents visit, they learn about and observe the intelligences in action.

9. **Parents as Intelligence Specialists:** Parents describe their careers to demonstrate how intelligences are used outside the classroom.

10. **School Work Nights:** Parents prepare art materials, help with student projects, or other MI tasks identified by the "family" teachers.

11. **Open Houses:** Family groupings invite parents to school at the end of thematic units or Theater of Learning classes.

—Adapted from Desombre (1997).

TEACHING PARENTS ABOUT MI

Parents, both old and new, are supportive of EXPO. In fact, the primary reason for the school's growth is parental requests for admission. Katrina Wentzel, a parent so impressed with EXPO's program that she later became the school's curriculum coordinator, tells of one such request: "A parent brought a 1st grade student to EXPO to enroll her. The girl had been diagnosed as learning disabled in reading and math. At the same time, she had perfect pitch and sang before she talked. Her parent explained, 'I want her at EXPO because she'll be seen for who she is.' The parent was right." According to Wentzel, the student is making good progress in the basic skills and excelling in music.

At EXPO, teachers have developed effective strategies for informing parents about MI and, subsequently, their children's education. Arlene Desombre, a member of the primary team, has compiled a list of ways EXPO parents learn about MI, shown in Figure 2.9.

Students are often excited to host their parents at school, and, as a result, Open Houses can be extravagant events. For example, at the Hmong Learning Theater Open House, parents encountered a three-dimensional Hmong village, Hmong storytelling and puppet shows, and traditional Hmong music and dancing. In fall 1998, several family groupings created Living History Museums, where EXPO students each studied a historical figure, dressed in character, and informed parents of the significance of the individual's life and contributions. Such events generate much student and parental enthusiasm for attending school.

Parental involvement at EXPO takes many forms. Parents serve on the Site-Based Decision-Making Council and its committees and attend "family" events; hundreds volunteer every year. Another important approach to working with 35 percent of the school's parents who are non-English speakers is through the Hmong Parent/Teacher Organization. EXPO's goal is to make everyone a significant member of the school's "family." In fact, EXPO teachers no longer refer to themselves as "teachers" but, rather, as "family educators." As Principal Paul Osterlund explains, "We embrace the responsibility of educating our families as well as our students. We work to create a close and explicit relationship that produces extraordinary results."

While teachers call themselves "family educators," many parents call them "miracle workers." Parents appreciate the staff's skills at identifying student strengths and making each child successful. The demand for enrollment at EXPO and the strong parental support appear to result from the school's ability to engage parents in multiple ways just as it engages its students.

MI ASSESSMENT APPROACHES

Since EXPO's inception, MI teaching techniques have been embedded in the school's curriculum, as have performance assessment measures. Assessment is as varied as the multiple intelligences: portfolios, audiotapes, written reports, teacher observations and narratives, student projects, presentations and performances, interviews, teacher-made tests, checklists, videos, student course and self-evaluations, standardized tests, and parent feedback. To foster intrinsic motivation, EXPO does not award letter grades, emphasizing instead that the best is expected from everyone: students, teachers, support staff, and administrators. Expecting excellence is the norm at EXPO for Excellence Elementary School.

The high expectations positively affect students. Family educator Terri Webber describes some of her expectations for primary students: "I expect my students to be self-directed and creative. They have to present in front of others and as a result they develop self-confidence. I expect a lot because they've proven they can do a lot." Fellow primary teacher, Anne McNeill, observes how learning and assessment shift from being teacher-directed to student-directed. "I provide ideas at the beginning. Then I let the kids show me the ways that they like to learn. As the year goes on, they create their own performance-assessments." Even at a school where "we see every child as gifted," says Curriculum Coordinator Katrina Wentzel, "sometimes we are surprised by the strengths we see emerge." EXPO students meet and, at times, exceed their teachers' expectations of excellence.

WORK SAMPLING EVALUATION

EXPO uses an assessment program called the Work Sampling System, developed by Samuel Meisels (1996/1997). It evaluates student performance in the context of everyday classroom learning. Because of this comprehensive approach, EXPO teachers claim that the program is a good match for their MI curriculum.

Work Sampling uses three forms of documentation: checklists, portfolios, and summary reports. The *checklists* describe the essential skills and knowledge that students should acquire in nearly all of the multiple intelligences: personal and social development, language and literacy, mathematical thinking, scientific thinking, social studies, the arts, and physical fitness. The checklists are helpful not only for assessment purposes but also as guides for

---

Figure 2.10

**Arts PROPEL Principles of Assessment Used by EXPO for Excellence
Elementary Magnet School**

1. Assessment captures growth over time.
2. Assessment is multidimensional, securing information from a variety of sources.
3. Assessment informs instruction.
4. Informal teacher assessment is important.
5. Students are active self-assessors.

---

lesson planning and instruction. Traditional divisions between assessment and instruction dissolve, because the data from instruction are the data of assessment.

Portfolios, the second form of documentation in the Work Sampling method, contrast with many student portfolios now in use. Instead of compiling samples of student work, EXPO's portfolios are structured collections that show growth over time. Both students and teachers select items that indicate progress in mastering the content and skills specified in the checklists. In addition, the portfolios document each child's goals, interests, and abilities. All portfolio entries are taken from daily classroom work, such as solving math problems, playing the piano, writing a story, or using conflict negotiating skills. Entries may be in the form of written work, audiotapes, videotapes, and drawings.

At EXPO, *summary reports* have replaced traditional report cards. The reports synthesize information from teacher observations, checklists, and portfolios into evaluations of student performance in all intelligences. Teachers complete the reports three times a year by writing narratives of student progress and completing rating scales.

Work Sampling at EXPO puts into practice many assessment principles identified by Howard Gardner and other researchers at Harvard Project Zero and Educational Testing Service (1991), as well as teachers and students in Pittsburgh, Cambridge, and Boston. Between 1986 and 1991, the researchers studied assessment in the humanities and the arts, concluding that evaluation should be guided by five basic principles of assessment. These principles are the assessment basics of Harvard Project Zero's Arts PROPEL (see Figure 2.10). These five principles are incorporated into the Work Sampling Method of evaluation. EXPO piloted Work Sampling for the St. Paul School District, and the method is now being adopted districtwide.

STUDENT ACHIEVEMENT

The 720 K–6 students at EXPO for Excellence Elementary Magnet School are a diverse group, as mentioned in the school demographics section. Fifty percent are minority, 10 percent are special-needs students, 35 percent are Hmong ESL students, and 50 percent are on free and reduced lunch. With the typical profile of many inner-city schools, EXPO students have made atypical and impressive scores on the standardized Metropolitan Achievement Tests (MATs) and the criterion-referenced Minnesota Comprehensive Assessment Tests.

To perceive EXPO's test scores in a broader context, it is helpful to consider how counterparts fare in urban schools across the country. *Education Week's* 1998 *Quality Counts* report states, "Urban students perform far worse, on average, than children who live outside central cities on virtually every measure of academic performance." The report goes on to explain that more than half of the 4th graders in urban public districts fail to achieve minimum standards in basic skills on standardized tests. Additionally, when the majority of students at an urban school are poor, two thirds or more likely are not performing at grade level.

Against this backdrop, EXPO student achievement is remarkable. As Principal Paul Osterlund explains: "What our test scores show is that 75 percent of the students who have been at EXPO for a minimum of three years or more score at or above average on the MAT tests. These scores are among the highest in St. Paul. This result is all the more notable because we do not teach to the test. We teach our curriculum."

Additional MAT data on student achievement at EXPO shows that in 1996, 36 percent of the students scored above average, increasing to 38 percent in 1997. In 1998, Minnesota administered its first series of standards-based, criterion-referenced basic skills tests. Third and 5th grade students were tested in math and reading. The math assessments included problems involving shape, space and measurement, number sense, and chance and data handling. The reading assessment consisted of three types of passages: literary, textbook, and practical knowledge such as recipes or glossaries. In addition to math and reading, 5th graders were also tested in writing by responding to a single prompt. Though this was their first encounter with such tests, similar to their performance on the MAT, EXPO students performed well. Third graders scored above the district average in both math and reading. Likewise, 5th graders scored above the district average in math, reading, and writing.

EXPO students significantly outperform their peers locally and across the country. These results, as good as they are, however, are not necessarily acceptable to the staff at EXPO. As the principal explains, "Even though they [the test scores] are favorable, we are not enamored with any assessment statistics, because the MAT tests do not reflect the work we do at the school."

Standardized tests to measure the MI achievement of EXPO students have not been developed. Nevertheless, with the traditional MAT tests and the newer state assessments, EXPO scores are so consistently high that many in the St. Paul School District have asked, "What are you doing right?" The staff has a ready answer to this question. They are offering an MI program that is right for EXPO students and perhaps for many others.

MIDDLE-LEVEL SCHOOLS, MI, AND STUDENT ACHIEVEMENT

3

"Teachers definitely need to let kids experience all the intelligences, because we're not what we thought we were and we keep changing."

—9th grade student
Skyview Junior High School, Bothell, Washington

"Why does it take people so long to figure it out? MI should spread like wildfire. The real gamble in education is doing the same old thing."

—Patricia Bolanos, founder and principal
Key Learning Community, Indianapolis, Indiana

The two schools described in this chapter exhibit striking contrasts and similarities. The first, Skyview Junior High, is a large, suburban junior high school of 900 students. By contrast, Key Learning Community is a small, urban public middle school with 165 students in grades 6–8. Skyview serves a middle-class community; nearly half of Key Learning Community's student population is below the poverty level. There is relatively little diversity at Skyview and much at Key.

Although the differences between the schools are significant, their similarities are remarkable. They are among the first middle-level MI schools in the nation. Both were founded by teachers and administrators who, dissatisfied with conventional approaches to schooling, wanted to create enhanced models of middle-level education and achievement. At these two exemplary schools,

- Student achievement outdistances that of comparable schools in their local communities.
- Teachers practice their beliefs faithfully.

Figure 3.1

A Snapshot of Two Middle-Level School MI Programs

SCHOOL, LOCATION, DATE FOUNDED	STUDENT DEMOGRAPHICS	MI INSTRUCTION	MI ASSESSMENT	UNIQUE MI FEATURES
Skyview Junior High School Bothell, Washington Founded in 1992.	Suburban school with 900 students in 7th, 8th, and 9th grades. Ten percent are minority, and 10 percent are on free and reduced lunch.	Interdisciplinary teams of teachers teach grade-level communities. Daily electives enable students to develop talents in-depth.	School uses a mixture of performance-based and traditional classroom assessments. On Comprehensive Test of Basic Skills (CTBS), 8th graders score 20 percent-age points higher than state and national peers.	Students choose acceleration classes for in-depth intelligence development. Breakout! project conducted by 9th graders, who use their talents to better their community.
Key Learning Community Indianapolis, Indiana Middle school added to K–5 program in 1993.	Inner-city school of 165 6th, 7th, and 8th graders. Nearly 50 percent are minority, and 44 percent are on free and reduced lunch.	Uses a thematic, multi-age program that dedicates equal time to all eight intelligences. Teachers are intelligence specialists.	Videotaped projects reflect student growth over time. School uses its own MI-based report card. On state and national tests, students achieve above grade level in all areas.	School program is organized around MI outcomes. Remediation is replaced with enrichment. Students develop areas of talent through pod electives, projects, and mentoring.

Figure 3.1 provides a snapshot of the middle school and junior high school featured in this chapter.

Skyview Junior High School in Bothell, Washington

School Demographics

Skyview Junior High School is 15 miles north of downtown Seattle. The largest of six junior high schools in the Northshore School District, drawing from a middle-class community, Skyview serves over 900 7th, 8th, and 9th graders. Ten percent of the school's population receives free and reduced lunch, and 10 percent are minority students. The school's 43 teachers are organized in grade-level teams, and class size averages 29 students.

Why MI?

In response to its rapid suburban growth, the Northshore School District scheduled the opening of a new junior high school for September 1992. In 1991, a planning team was formed to design the curriculum. Team members soon identified a single, critical question that any junior high school program should address: "How can we best meet the needs of the adolescent?"

During their initial meetings, some members of the planning group, familiar with MI, explained the theory to their colleagues. They asserted that MI was appropriate for adolescents, with its identification of personal and social intelligences and its implications for active learning. The rest of the team members agreed. From its inception, Skyview's mission and curriculum were anchored in MI theory and practice.

Creating an MI Program

Skyview Junior High took three steps to become an MI site. First, in 1991, the planning team announced the school's MI focus. Fortunately, the concept was well received by numerous stakeholders: new colleagues hired to teach at the site, district personnel, the broader educational community, parents, and even the construction workers building the new facility. The enthusiastic embrace of the school's mission was physically symbolized in a large mural of the original seven intelligences painted high on the wall of the school's cafeteria.

Having made the MI commitment, however, team members soon realized their pioneering status. No other known secondary MI program existed. Lacking models to guide their design efforts, a necessary second step was to undertake extensive professional development. Team members and the school's new teachers read Gardner's books and articles, created a professional library, attended conferences and workshops, and hired MI consultants for staff development.

Third, the planning team created Skyview's schedule. To emphasize the personal intelligences, team members suggested forming grade-level learning communities. Interdisciplinary teams of English, math, science, and social studies teachers would teach and advise in 7th, 8th, or 9th grade learning communities. The teams determined that the use of interdisciplinary blocks would enable them to accommodate special-needs students in the school's program. They also decided to offer P.E. and "acceleration" classes daily.

The acceleration class was created, literally, to accelerate the development of students' intelligences. During this hour, students would attend clubs, pursue enrichment activities, learn about multimedia, and receive extra study support to increase academic achievement. Believing that students should acquire lifelong learning skills, the team also recommended the use of extensive grade-level projects to emphasize self-directed learning.

With the school's major curricular components identified, the planning team's final task was to write a mission statement. The one they crafted drew upon Gardner's problem-solving definition of human intelligence:

Gateway to My Universe

Skyview students will discover the gateway to their learning potential through demonstrating personal responsibility by meeting the standards of quality work; demonstrating appropriate, productive behavior in the school community; and developing the ability to think and solve problems at school and apply that knowledge to situations encountered in their lives.

Skyview Junior High School was ready to open in September 1992.

THE MI CURRICULUM

"The team-based, MI approach at our school," says Skyview's Principal Holly Call, "raises the collective intelligence of all staff. The teams' ongoing problem solving leads to enriched offerings for our students."

The enriched offerings for students include seven-period days for 7th and 8th graders, and three blocks daily for 9th graders, who use the extended time for in-depth research and scholarship. Teachers are assigned to specific grade levels and work in teams. Teams have the same planning time daily to discuss student concerns and to develop interdisciplinary curriculum. With MI at the school's core, teachers also employ common vocabulary, belief systems, and goals.

Team members serve as "intelligence experts" for one another. In planning a fiction unit, for example, an English teacher might learn how logic is structured into a storyline from a math colleague and how to explain a physics principle mentioned in a novel from a science teacher. Together, the teams also select Washington State standards to highlight in instruction and assessment.

Another team function is to identify ways to bolster individual student or group achievement. Technology teacher John Moen says he is impressed with "a culture of respect for and belief in all students," which is evident at faculty meetings. John attributes this respect for students, including those who struggle the most, to the teachers' beliefs in MI. Teachers intentionally observe students from several perspectives and, in so doing, perceive intellectual strengths and academic possibilities.

Mirroring their teachers, students contribute to the culture of respect. As a 9th grader explains: "It's fun when you recognize that friends have different intelligences, and, in fact, the friends I appreciate the most have strengths different than mine. At this school, we make a lot of friends because we all help each other."

The outcomes of such attitudes are significant. As Laurie Nunnelee, a 9th grade teacher, explains, "There are many instances of reluctant students turning around and 'checking back in.' "

FORMULA-LESS MI TEACHING

In their individual classrooms, teachers rarely use specialized MI grids for lesson planning. Because MI has driven the school from its inception, some teachers wonder whether the theory or their beliefs came first. Instead of reworking content in seven or eight modes, the teachers diversify instruction. Academic content dictates the intelligences most relevant for each lesson.

For example, "Genetics: Who Am I?", a 7th grade science and math unit, illustrates this natural integration of content and multimodal instruction. While the logical intelligences predominate, the three-week unit also draws upon linguistic and artistic intelligences. Students read about genetics, observe simulations of DNA, write essays and poems on nature versus nurture, and create murals of their genetic identities. In math, they study probability to explore variations among traits and consider questions such as, "What is the chance of an individual having brown eyes?"

AN MI-RICH TOTAL SCHOOL PROGRAM

In addition to integrated units, students develop their multifaceted potential through the schoolwide program and daily acceleration classes. Acceleration serves as enrichment for every student. During acceleration, students delve into an area of promise, explore new interests, or strengthen academic weaknesses. Teachers teach the accelerated classes according to their interests and talents. Options include:

Technology Design Club	Art Club
Fitness Training	Choir
Pep Band	Honor Society
Math Club	Talent Show
Newspaper	School Governance
Peer Mediation	Geography Bee
Natural Helpers	Multimedia Exploration Club
Media Literacy Club	Sports
Computer/Web Club	

Originally scheduled during the regular school day, acceleration, by student request, was moved to after school hours. As of the 1998-99 school year, students have two hours of enriched, activity-based opportunities. They also have access to the library, computer lab, peer study groups, and core teachers; many use the extended period to serve as peer tutors.

GETTING PERSONAL

To respond to adolescents' interests and developmental needs, Skyview emphasizes the personal intelligences. Students spend their days in grade-level learning communities, where strong bonds are forged among peers and with teachers. Additionally, 8th graders attend week-long "personal success skills" seminars, and 9th graders conduct "Make a Difference" projects that link them with the broader community.

All 7th grade students are taught about MI theory, and, as a result, learn to perceive individual strengths as they gain appreciation for the diverse talents of their classmates. Though students are explicitly taught about MI upon entry to Skyview, the theory remains important throughout all three years. As a 9th grader commented, "Kids who learned about MI in 7th grade see themselves differently, and we become more confident over the years because of it."

Some media students are willing to put their confidence to the test by assuming the responsibility of producing the "Good Morning Skyview" broadcast. This live morning news program features anchors, sports, special-interest shorts, and personal montages. All intelligences are engaged and stretched, as students produce a daily television show for their peers and teachers.

BREAKOUT!

Perhaps the most remarkable MI feature at Skyview is the school's award-winning Breakout! program. Created by the 9th grade teachers, Breakout!, a yearlong program, requires each 9th grader to develop an intelligence strength and use that talent to benefit others. At Skyview, expertise is defined as making a difference in one's community.

Students ask community members to serve as mentors, and teacher-advisors track student progress and evaluate the project upon its completion. Students determine their projects' content and which intelligences they'll draw upon, but teachers specify the skills to be demonstrated: Students must apply the knowledge and skills acquired during the previous two years at the school. For example, in 7th and 8th grade English classes, students learn to conduct interviews, write letters, take notes, outline information, and use bibliographic formats. In social studies, they conduct research and practice diverse problem-solving strategies. In math and science, they analyze data and interpret statistics. In P.E., self-assessments help them establish personalized goals, and, in art, they acquire design and performance techniques. By 9th grade, Skyview students are expected to use all of these skills in highly polished ways.

The Breakout! program is organized with student "passports," which list the required skills in all subject areas and the dates for completion. For example, English skills required for a successful Breakout! project include interviewing, letter-writing, note-taking, employing correct bibliographic form, public speaking, journaling, writing pamphlets, and using the thinking skills of detecting bias, comparing and contrasting, and evaluating sources. Required art skills consist of identifying a medium, creating a materials list, preplanning a design, and using high-quality craftsmanship in execution. Other subjects and their specific skills are listed in the 20+ page passport each student receives. The first two pages of a Skyview passport are shown in Figure 3.2. They illustrate general questions about a presentation and key due dates.

Figure 3.2

Sample Pages from Skyview Junior High School's Breakout! Project Passport

	Advisor's Stamp		Due Dates:	
What is your focus?				Final topic selection
What is your message?				Preliminary plan
List your strongest intelligence areas:				Community connection Preliminary annotated bibliography and notes
Which intelligence area will you use to convey your message?				Final annotated bibliography and notes
What are you going to do to make a difference?				Performance ready Last day for pamphlets in computer lab
				Presentation week
				Celebration night

—*Reproduced with permission of Skyview Junior High School.*

Students live up to the high expectations of Breakout! Not only do they demonstrate mastery of important skills, but they reveal an eagerness to contribute to their community. Skyview students are frequently seen volunteering in hospitals, nursing homes, or schools. Others make works of art, do presentations, produce videos, or write computer programs. Still others promote causes, such as instituting an Arthur Ashe Day, spearheading a local wetlands rehabilitation project, or creating a CD to raise funds for a new performance center.

Originally, Breakout! was based on the multiple intelligences, but the project has evolved so that MI is implicit in it. Several intelligences are engaged through the required disciplinary work and from teachers' and students' suggestions of numerous ways to complete project components. As a 9th grader explains, "We learned about MI in 7th grade, but it was most useful in 9th. I could not have done my Breakout! project so smoothly if I didn't know about MI. It gave me so many options."

Parents as Team Members

While parents were not involved in Skyview's early planning stages, they have become increasingly knowledgeable and supportive of the school's philosophy and approach. Many parents are first introduced to MI theory by their children. Typically, the 7th graders talk to their parents about MI after learning about it at school.

More formal ways of involving parents in the school's program have evolved. To ensure easy communication between school and home, an element frequently lacking in many secondary schools, parents are teamed with the same interdisciplinary core of teachers who work with their children. Parents are invited to team conferences to discuss concerns about their child or to participate in curricular planning. Other linkages include parent/teacher meetings, the school newspaper, an active PTSA, a Parent Communication Network, and attendance at special events, such as Breakout! evening presentations.

Additionally, each year parents hold a Career Awareness Day featuring about 30 professions. They also work in classrooms as acceleration mentors, or volunteer in the health room, library, or computer lab. Some assist with emergency preparedness, others design and publish the school's newspaper, and still others organize school assemblies. Such extensive parental involvement at the secondary level may help to explain why in 1997 600 Skyview students were acknowledged by their teacher teams for excellence in scholarship and effort.

Student Achievement

Classroom assessment at Skyview is not explicitly MI-based, but is often performance-based, as evident in Breakout! Typically, teachers use rubrics to grade exhibitions, demonstrations, visuals, and music presentations. However, if an objective in language arts is effective essay writing, then students will undergo some legitimate and demanding assessment. Though teachers appreciate multiple forms of giftedness, they, nevertheless, as one claims, do not "cut students any slack" in the basics. Talented athletes or musicians, for example, cannot justify weak performances in reading. Instead, teachers and students identify weaknesses and set goals to work harder in those areas. Further, Skyview teachers proactively address each grade level's specific academic needs. Once a year, teacher teams survey their grade level's performance and, subsequently, adjust their curriculum to target the greatest academic needs.

STANDARDIZED TEST ACHIEVEMENT

Standardized student achievement at Skyview has been measured by the Comprehensive Test of Basic Skills (CTBS), a state-mandated test given to 4th and 8th grade students each October. In 1998, this test was replaced by the Iowa Test of Basic Skills (ITBS). Since 1993, Skyview has raised test scores consistently in all core areas, even though the school is the only one of the district's five junior highs housing three levels of special-needs students: profound and medically fragile, self-contained, and those included in the regular classroom. Similarly, Skyview students outperform their state and national peers by 20 percentage points in reading, language arts, and math. Teachers attribute student achievement to the school's shared belief in and commitment to developing the multiple intelligences.

ACHIEVEMENT ON WASHINGTON ASSESSMENT OF STUDENT LEARNING TESTS

In contrast to the multiple-choice format of the standardized CTBS tests, Washington State has developed its own performance-based measures. These tests require students to write descriptive essays, compare information from different texts, use math skills to solve complex problems, and explain the thinking behind their answers. In the spring of 1998, the Washington Assessment of Student Learning (WASL) tests were administered for the first time to middle or junior high school students. Held to new and higher standards, most students throughout the state did not perform well. Skyview was an exception. In the four categories tested, Skyview students scored higher than the five other junior high schools in the Northshore School District. This is particularly interesting because the student demographics of Skyview match those of another junior high, which had the lowest scores in the district. The table in Figure 3.3 compares Skyview students' achievement with their peers across the state. While the pilot year test results reveal much room for improvement, Skyview students already have a head start on test performance. Principal Holly Call has one explanation for the school's scores: "I believe our students scored as well as they did the first time through because of our multiple intelligences program."

Though strong student achievement is a reward in itself, Skyview has received additional rewards from its MI program. Breakout! received a Washington Education Association's Leaders in Restructuring Award, and

Figure 3.3

Achievement of Skyview Junior High School Students and Their Peers on the Washington Assessment of Student Learning (WASL) Tests

Essential Area Tested	Percentage of Washington State students meeting the WASL standards	Percentage of Skyview's students meeting the WASL standards
Reading	38.4%	61.5%
Writing	31.3%	48.6%
Math	20.1%	36.6%
Listening	80.2%	92.6%

teachers have won awards, grants, and recognition from national subject discipline groups. In 1998, Skyview received a $25,000 grant to improve its "Good Morning Skyview" MI media program. The updated lab will serve the community as a video production center for local businesses and parents. In addition, administrators and teachers have been asked to present their school's program at local, state, and national conferences, and educators from around the United States and beyond have visited Skyview. The school is a model to others seeking to develop secondary MI programs, just as the original Skyview planning team did in 1991.

Perhaps some of the greatest rewards are more subtle. Student descriptions of their educational experiences are affirming. In October 1998, the staff held a retreat to reflect on and assess their MI program. Some of the presenters included Skyview graduates who described the benefits of their MI junior high experiences. For example, one claimed, "Skyview set me up for the rest of my school career because I know my strengths." Teachers at the local high school have noticed differences between Skyview students and those from other junior highs. They report that Skyview grads consistently sit in the front of the classroom. This simple, nonverbal message reveals Skyview students' eagerness to learn and their belief that they can.

KEY LEARNING COMMUNITY
IN INDIANAPOLIS, INDIANA

SCHOOL DEMOGRAPHICS

The Key Learning Community is a public elementary and middle school in Indianapolis, Indiana, housed in one building. The elementary school is on the first floor, and the middle school is on the second. The middle school has 10 teachers for its 165 6th, 7th, and 8th grade students. The demographics of Key middle schoolers mirror those of their peers in the rest of the city: nearly half are minority students, and 44 percent are on free and reduced lunch.

The Key middle-level program began in 1993 as an extension of the Key School, the first U.S. elementary school centered on Gardner's theory of multiple intelligences. Less than 50 percent of the middle-level students, however, come from Key's elementary program. With 500 students on a waiting list, Key Learning Community plans to evolve into a K–12 site. Serving as a citywide magnet, the school is unusual in that it maintains no academic requirements for admission. Students are selected by lottery, and although some who choose Key are already identified as gifted and talented, the others discover their gifts and talents while attending the school.

CREATING AN MI PROGRAM

In 1984, the founding teachers of the Key School were working together at a large elementary school in Indianapolis. Plans for significant restructuring had been under way, with the "Key Crew" strongly supporting schoolwide change. When it became evident, however, that little change would occur, the Key teachers became disenchanted and soon, in effect, seceded from the school.

In the intervening two years before opening their own magnet program, the "Key Crew," also known as the "Indianapolis Eight," lobbied their district, discussed their beliefs, developed curriculum, raised funds, met with Howard Gardner, and received approval to begin an inner-city, "options" elementary school. A small art deco building was identified as the school site for the 1987–88 year. Part of the power of the Key School derives from the fact that it was teacher initiated with top administrative support.

Over the next few years, as students progressed through the elementary grades, parents questioned what would happen to their children's learning in traditional junior high schools. These parental concerns led Key teachers to consider extending their program. They originally hoped to link their program with existing secondary schools in Indianapolis. Unsuccessful at forging new collaborations, the Key staff found themselves in a position similar to the one they encountered in the mid-1980s. Their reaction was the same as in 1991: to open their own school. After two years of planning, lobbying, and fundraising, Key Renaissance Middle School opened in 1993. The staff now plans to add a grade level each year until the school becomes a K–12 site, probably in 2002. In 1997, the school combined its elementary and middle-level programs to become the Key Learning Community. Since the school's inception, Pat Bolanos has served as Key's principal.

THE MI CURRICULUM

Key's program is based on a thematic, community-oriented, MI curriculum. The school's credo claims that students have the "right to develop their multiple intelligences." To actualize this right, the school provides an "equitable" education. Pat Bolanos explains, "Every student in our learning community is given equal access to every area we teach." Subsequently, all middle school students take English, German, instrumental music, math, science, visual arts, physical education, and geography/history.

In addition to the common curriculum, learning is personalized at Key by parents, teachers, and community members who offer elective classes and mentoring experiences. While all staff teach *through* the intelligences, the school's total curricular program teaches *for* intelligence.

MI OUTCOMES

Key Learning Community expects students to be literate in all intelligences and to develop their individual talents in depth. To demonstrate this commitment, the school is perhaps the first in the nation to identify MI educational outcomes, which specify the essential tasks, achievements, and habits of mind all Key students should demonstrate. Upon graduation, each Key student will

- Communicate clearly in written form
- Be verbally articulate in two languages
- Sing or play a musical instrument proficiently
- Use math and logic in applied areas
- Use technology as a tool for inquiry and communication
- Recreate the three-dimensional world through the visual or practical arts

- Be physically fit
- Select an applied area for inquiry, reflection, and apprenticeship
- Participate in stewardship activities with nature
- Express a capacity to care about global issues
- Participate in groups and organizations in the larger community.

For students to achieve such outcomes, the teachers must be unified in their beliefs and their pedagogy. Contrary to many schools, where teachers function independently of one another, the Key staff works collectively. Their likemindedness is evident in the explicit requirements for employment and retention at the school. To become and remain a member of the staff, each teacher agrees to apply MI theory in instruction; collaborate with colleagues; teach and assess thematic, multi-age programs; reflect on one's practice; keep abreast of research; and actively work with students and others on community service. These criteria for employment are translated into Key's weekly schedule, schoolwide themes, and ongoing teacher professional development.

AN MI-BASED WEEKLY SCHEDULE

Students from 6th through 8th grade attend Key from 8:30 until 3:30 daily. As is evident in the schedule shown in Figure 3.4, students take courses that encompass all intelligences.

What is not evident is the school's stance that students be taught by experts in their disciplines. As English teacher Beth Lively emphasizes, "Each middle school teacher at Key is a specialist in her field." According to Principal Pat Bolanos, teacher specialists demand more of their students. For example, in the middle school art classroom, students are expected to knowledgeably discuss the following topics:

- Why does art exist?
- Where does art come from?
- What is considered art?
- How do different cultures practice art?

Contrary to most middle school schedules, each subject at Key is taught for 200 minutes weekly. Such parity reveals the school's view that each form of intelligence is as important as every other. All students study the same core curriculum featuring basic academics, second language learning, the arts, and technology instruction. One 7th grade student explains what she appreciates most about Key: "Everything has equal time, and all subjects are equal." Another expands upon these thoughts, "One of the best things about Key is that there is more time for things like art and gym than at other schools. The teachers here are more involved too, and students help each other more."

The weekly schedule includes both single and double classes. Students begin each day in small advisory groups, which function as a home base.

			Figure 3.4		
		Key Learning Community Middle School Schedule			
	MONDAY	TUESDAY	WEDNESDAY	THURSDAY	FRIDAY
8:30	Early arrival breakfast	Early arrival breakfast	Early arrival breakfast	Early arrival breakfast	Early arrival breakfast
8:55	Advisory	Advisory	Advisory	Advisory	Advisory
9:20	P.E.	Boys' P.E. Girls' science	Girls' P.E. Boys' science	Boys' P.E. Girls' science	Girls' P.E. Boys' science
9:55	Science	Boys' P.E. Girls' science	Girls' P.E. Boys' science	Boys' P.E. Girls' science	Girls' P.E. Boys' science
10:30	Linguistics	Linguistics	Music	Linguistics	Music
11:05	Music	Linguistics	Music	Linguistics	Music
11:40	Lunch and presentations	Lunch and pod elective	Lunch and pod elective	Lunch and pod elective	Lunch and pod elective
1:10	Art	Boys' math Girls' art	Girls' math Boys' art	Boys' math Girls' art	Girls' math Boys' art
1:45	Math	Boys' math Girls' art	Girls' math Boys' art	Boys' math Girls' art	Girls' math Boys' art
2:20	Geography/ history	Geography/ history	German	Geography/ history	German
2:55	German	Geography/ history	German	Geography/ history	German
3:30	Clean-up, dismissal	Clean-up, dismissal	Clean-up, dismissal	Clean-up, dismissal	Clean-up, dismissal

—Reproduced with permission of Key Learning Community.

Advisory groups meet later in the day during elective time to reinforce close teacher-student ties.

On Mondays, the school's schedule consists of single class sessions. The week also begins with a community member who demonstrates a craft or skill of interest to the K–8 students. Parents are often the guest presenters, and they make an effort to integrate their expertise with the school's current theme.

On Tuesdays through Fridays, the schedule switches from single to double periods. Two of the subjects, math and physical education, are gender-grouped. Key teachers assert that such classes accommodate the varying developmental needs of female and male adolescents. Another noteworthy feature of Tuesdays through Fridays at Key is "pods," the only elective courses that students pursue.

POD ELECTIVES

The pod electives are named after the phrase "peas in a pod." Pods are designed and taught by teachers and attended by any interested K-8 student. Because of the multi-age groupings, students work comfortably at their own pace and developmental levels.

The teachers at Key philosophically oppose remedial education. Instead, they staunchly focus on enriching each student's area of promise. The pods are one way the school develops student talent. At the same time, if a student is struggling in an intelligence area, tutoring is provided until skills are improved.

During any school year as many as 12 pods may be offered. To organize pods, teachers write descriptions of electives they would like to offer. Students select their top three choices and are guaranteed assignment in one of the three. Students remain in their pods all year for in-depth skill and knowledge development. One student explained that pod was her favorite class because "it lets me do what I like best with friends who have the same interests." In 1998, students could select from among 11 pods in computers, choir, art, careers, explorers, fitness, poetry, stitchery, Now and Then (history), Theater and Backstage, or Walk Indy (a walking tour of the city of Indianapolis).

At the middle school level, pods connect Key adolescents with real-world responsibilities. Advised by their pod teachers, 6th through 8th grade students conduct community service projects throughout Indianapolis. For example, during the Walk Indy Pod, students visited a homeless shelter and a farmers' market. Reflecting upon the two field trips, the students created a community service project: making vegetable soup for the homeless. Such projects challenge Key students to give of their talents for the common good. The Key staff hypothesizes that youthful community involvement will encourage adolescents to surpass the accomplishments of those before them and inspire service as future city leaders.

Such leadership goals are further reinforced by the 8th grade mentoring program. Key employs a full-time service and mentor teacher, Kathy Calwell, who fulfills Gardner's suggested school role of "a community broker." The responsibilities of this position include pairing students with community role models. To initiate this process, the mentor teacher interviews 8th grade students about their interests. She then identifies business people, professors, doctoral students, artists, and other willing volunteer mentors. To forge the actual matches, the "brokering" teacher schedules a meeting with a student, his or her parents, and the community member. When a match appears likely, all parties specify the expectations and responsibilities of the mentoring experience. Through this program, every 8th grade student receives one-on-one mentoring from a community expert.

Kathy Calwell explains how the mentoring process works: "Each 8th grader has a mentor in his or her strength, an area of curiosity, or in a career interest. The students meet once a week with their mentors. They actually go to work with them and do projects with them. Students spend two hours a week at work with their mentors some of whom are architects, firefighters, attorneys, artists, and university professors."

The benefits of mentoring are clearly evident to students. "My mentor makes me feel important," explains one 8th grader, "and he gives me an idea of what a career is like."

When Key adds its future 9th through 12th grades, the middle school mentoring program will transform into high school apprenticeships. Plans for enhancing each student's potential do not end here, however. The school envisions a continuum of talent development that unfolds in sequence: from pods, to community service, to mentoring, to apprenticeships, to postsecondary training and study, and onto meaningful careers. Once engaged in their careers, the Key staff hopes its graduates will remain in Indianapolis as city leaders dedicated to improving the quality of life for all its citizens.

THEMATIC PROJECTS

Key students conduct major projects related to each of the school's yearly themes. In the projects, students are required to display content knowledge and skills, as well as reveal their individual interests and talents. During their

Figure 3.5

Thematic Project Self-Reflection Questions for Key Learning Community Students

- Explain how the project relates to the school theme.
- Explain your reasons for selecting the project topic.
- Describe the quality of your multimodal presentations.
- Specify how you will use the information from this project in the future.
- Identify the impact of the project on you as a learner.
- Explain how you will improve your self-directed learning.
- Identify the most outstanding aspect of your project.

—Reproduced with permission of Key Learning Community.

elementary years, teachers and parents guide students through all stages of project implementation. By middle school, however, students are expected to acquire self-directed learning skills. They are responsible for the initiation, implementation, refinement, presentation, reflection on, and assessment of all aspects of their projects.

At the end of each theme period, students present their projects to one another. These multimodal presentations deepen and extend learning because students perceive numerous facets of each theme through their classmates' work. In addition to their presentations, students submit written reports and self-assessments of their work. The self-assessments require in-depth reflection. Students are asked to respond to several questions (see Figure 3.5). The projects are demanding but, nevertheless, students enjoy them. As one 7th grader explains, "I work hard on my projects. They give me chances to show what I've learned in ways that are fun for me."

In addition to teaching autonomous learning skills, the projects serve as important assessment tools. Each presentation is videotaped by the staff video specialist, who archives them for ready access. During a school year, students have two or three new presentations added to their tapes and, at the end of middle school, they have six to nine presentations captured on tape.

The videos are used for a number of purposes. Students and parents watch them because they are entertaining and provide tangible evidence of academic achievement. Teachers use them to learn about their students. The tapes also ensure program accountability, as they clearly reveal student competencies. Over time, they show the evolution of students' talents and, many times, their career interests. Ultimately, each student accumulates a video portfolio that chronicles his or her cognitive development throughout the years at Key.

STAFF COLLABORATION

Just as Key students benefit from the expertise of others, so too do the teachers. The school's complex program depends upon extensive collegial interaction. Principal Bolanos has a formula for Key's model: "The starting point for an effective school program depends upon teacher discussion, collaboration, and professional development. The people who plan it must be the ones who do it." At Key, teachers discuss their curricular plans and assist one another in refining their professional practice.

THEMATIC PLANNING

Each year, two or three schoolwide themes are taught in 12-week blocks. Because much of the curriculum is thematically driven, the community has a lot at stake when choosing themes and, as a result, has evolved democratic processes for decision making. To identify the themes, school staff solicit ideas from parents, staff, students, visitors, and mentors during the school year. All suggestions are compiled and deliberated. At staff meetings, teachers speak on behalf of their preferred themes. In early spring, they vote for three preferred themes. The ones receiving the highest number of points are selected for implementation during the next school year. Previous years' themes have included "Changes in Time and Space," "The Renaissance: Past and Present," "Let's Make a Difference," and "Working in Harmony in Nature."

The timing of Key's theme selection process is intentional. Everyone's opinion is voiced, and the teachers have summer vacation to develop curriculum. Not all planning is done independently, however. The school's organizational structure accommodates extensive collaboration. Twice monthly, teachers meet to co-plan their units. At these meetings, they brainstorm student learning processes, identify the connections among their disciplines, use Gardner's eight intelligences to reflect on their individual classroom practice, and specify areas for professional growth. They also schedule dates when students will present their theme-related projects to their classmates.

PORTFOLIO PROJECTS FOR KEY TEACHERS

As of 1996, Key teachers have embraced a new project for themselves: professional portfolios. Twice monthly, the teachers hold forums to discuss beliefs and research that guide their practice. At the forums they also present lesson plans and classroom videotapes that document their efforts at improving instruction. All teachers at Key strive for professional mastery by identifying concrete instructional goals, brainstorming with colleagues about how to attain those goals, and reflecting on classroom results.

Key teachers assist one another with professional growth, providing honest, constructive feedback. While some may find such peer review daunting, Key teachers appear to thrive with such a collaborative process. English teacher Beth Lively claims, "There is no cookie-cutter approach here. I am treated as a professional, and I have greater confidence." Principal Bolanos gives an example of heightened teacher confidence in action: "Two Key teachers have been asked and have accepted part-time teaching positions at local universities."

Teachers credit the portfolio forums with enhancing the professional culture of their school. As a result, peer coaching is the norm, and the improvement of student learning is the common goal. As evident in these efforts, Key staff not only maintain high expectations for their students, they maintain similarly high standards for themselves.

Key teachers believe that their school is unique but, even more important, that it is educationally sound. The visitors, many educational awards, and considerable media recognition reinforce those beliefs. The school's name, the Key Learning Community, reflects what transpires at the site: a community of learners pursuing rigorous, lifelong personal and professional growth.

STUDENT ACHIEVEMENT

Because Key Learning Community is dedicated to developing human intelligence, it is not surprising that this mission is reflected in the school's evaluation tools. Key assesses all eight intelligences through project videotapes, classroom portfolios, and performance-based methods. For example, in foreign language, students are assessed on how well they speak the language. Similarly in music, students reveal their proficiency by playing an instrument, and in English they must display their writing skills in poetry, stories, plays, and essays. These methods imitate real-world activities useful both in and outside of school. Students' intelligences are tapped and assessed directly through each particular medium, rather than limited to conventional linguistic and mathematical means.

STANDARDIZED ACHIEVEMENT SCORES

Key students must, nonetheless, take standardized tests required by their school district and the State of Indiana. These tests include the Indiana State Test of Educational Proficiencies (ISTEP) and the California Test of Basic

Skills (CTB). In 1993 when the middle school opened, 50 percent of its students came from other than the Key elementary program. Initially, little more than half of the middle schoolers scored as average on the state's test. For the first couple of years, the students and school adjusted to innovative curricular and assessment practices and to the reality of required multiple-choice state tests. During this time, the format of the ISTEP test also changed to include written responses and problem-solving skills similar to those emphasized at Key.

As of 1998, the middle school students exceeded district goals on the ISTEP. This is surprising because the school admits students through a lottery system. Composite scores were available for Key 6th and 8th grade students who performed at or above grade level in the basic skills. The scores are shown in Figure 3.6

Similar solid results have been achieved with the California Test of Basic Skills. In 1998, the composite score for all Key 6th graders was at a 7.7 grade level in reading, language arts, math, and social studies. Key 7th graders had composite scores at the 8th grade level or above in all areas tested. Similarly, composite scores on the CTB for Key 8th graders showed them performing at the 9.3 grade level. When asked why Key students perform well on standardized tests, Principal Bolanos attributed their success to teacher specialists who are highly qualified to teach in their disciplines and to the equal time given to all intelligences throughout the schoolwide program.

KEY'S PROGRESS REPORT

In spite of the strong performance of Key students on standardized measures, the staff claims that such tests capture a narrow band of what Key students know and can do. To more accurately reflect the broad achievement profile of each student, the school developed its own Pupil Progress Report. Students are assessed in the eight intelligences through three criteria:

1. *Progress* refers to the rate of growth in an intelligence, which can be slow, steady, or rapid.
2. *Participation* describes whether a student is intrinsically or extrinsically motivated or passive or disruptive in class.
3. *Performance* refers to a developmental continuum.

Students may exhibit universal-level skills, or rudimentary awareness of the symbol systems; cultural-level skills, which consist of acquiring the basics of each subject area with modeling and guidance; and discipline-

Figure 3.6

**Key Learning Community's Scores on
1998 Indiana Statewide Testing for Educational Progress**

Grade and Number of Students	Grade Equivalent Reading Score Total	Grade Equivalent Language Score Total	Grade Equivalent Math Score Total
51 6th grade students	6.9	7.4	6.9
43 8th grade students	9.2	10.1	8.3

based performance, which indicates the degree of "literacy" in a discipline. Another unique feature of Key's Progress Report is that it specifies areas of exceptional promise, informing both student and parent of intelligence strengths that deserve enrichment.

All teachers contribute to each student's quarterly progress report. Once completed, they are discussed at mandatory parent, teacher, and student conferences. As with many features of the school, the Progress Report continues to evolve. In the future, Key students will self-assess their progress, participation, and performance on the reports once teachers have reached consensus about the criteria for student self-assessment.

ALIGNING BELIEFS

Key is used to being in the spotlight. It has been featured on television programs, such as "ABC World News Tonight with Peter Jennings" and PBS's "Why Do These Kids Love School?"; in videotapes, such as ASCD's *The Multiple Intelligences Series* and Phi Delta Kappa's *The Making of a School*; in such newspapers as *NEA Today* and *NUVO Newsweekly*; in books such as Gardner's *Multiple Intelligences: The Theory in Practice* and our own book, *Teaching and Learning Through Multiple Intelligences*; and in journals including *Educational Leadership, The NASSP Bulletin,* and *Child.* Thursdays of each week are scheduled to accommodate the hundreds of visitors who come each year to see MI in action. The staff also offers four-day summer institutes for educators wanting to learn more about Key's model.

When asked for advice about how to begin an MI program, Principal Bolanos has a ready-made answer. She explains that the first step is for all interested parties to discuss the ingrained assumptions, generalizations, or images that influence how they perceive students and how they teach. Beliefs left unexamined can serve as powerful obstacles to school, teacher, and student change. The converse is true, however. When beliefs are openly discussed and refined, they can move into alignment with every aspect of a school's work. When this occurs, schools that perceive the best in students are capable of getting the best from them, and MI creates a positive cycle of achievement.

4

HIGH SCHOOLS, MI, AND STUDENT ACHIEVEMENT

"I am morally obligated to act on my understanding of human intelligence."
—Eeva Reeder, math teacher
Mountlake Terrace High School, Mountlake Terrace, Washington

"Teachers no longer accept the idea that any student has an inability to learn."
—Norrie Bean, principal
Lincoln High School, Stockton, California

While MI theory has been embraced by many elementary and some middle schools, acceptance is rarer in high schools. This fact is puzzling because most comprehensive secondary programs have courses in all intelligences and teachers who can be identified as intelligence experts by the subjects they teach. The two schools described in this chapter—Lincoln High School in Stockton, California, and Mountlake Terrace High School in Mountlake Terrace, Washington—are similar to many high schools around the country. They are complex institutions with large departments and diverse programs. Also, like most large high schools, it is difficult to assign a single descriptor that applies to every teacher and department.

In our search for MI high schools of five or more years in duration for this book, Lincoln and Mountlake Terrace come close. Both high schools have numbers of teachers who have restructured teaching and learning based on MI theory. Both schools promote project-based learning, performance-based assessment, and the development of student intellectual talents. Because many teachers at Lincoln and Mountlake Terrace perceive students as multifaceted individuals, they have increased their demands for academic achievement—and students have responded accordingly. Figure 4.1 provides a snapshot of the two MI high school programs.

Figure 4.1

A Snapshot of Two MI High Schools

SCHOOL, LOCATION, AND DATE FOUNDED	STUDENT DEMOGRAPHICS	MI INSTRUCTION	MI ASSESSMENT	UNIQUE MI FEATURES
Mountlake Terrace High School Mountlake Terrace, Washington Opened in 1961 and adopted MI in 1990.	Suburban school with 1,865 students in 9th–12th grades. Twenty-five percent are minority, and 13% are on free and reduced lunch.	MI- and project-based classroom instruction. Three levels of disciplinary knowledge (replacing chronological grades) for in-depth understanding, yielding multi-age, continuous progress classes.	Performance-based assessments used in all classes. On state-mandated test, the Curriculum Framework Assessment System (CFAS), Terrace students outperform state peers in English, math, and social studies. On Scholastic Aptitude Test (SAT), they outperform state and national peers in math.	School program is organized around MI competencies. An Application Project, which requires mentoring by an expert and an exhibition to knowledgeable adults, is a prerequisite for graduation.
Lincoln High School Stockton, California Opened in 1954 and adopted MI in 1990.	Residential city school with 2,600 students in grades 9–12. Fifty percent are minority, 26% are on free and reduced lunch, and 13% are limited-English-speaking students.	MI-based classroom instruction is schoolwide. Several Integrated Studies courses offered from 9th–12th grades. Projects required in all classes.	Performance-based measures used in all classes. Extensive use of student self-assessment. Portfolio assessment in language arts. On Stanford Test of Academic Skills, school has the highest scores in its county. Ninety percent of graduates attend two- or four-year colleges.	School mission, beliefs, and strategies are dedicated to MI. Integrated Studies programs strive for in-depth disciplinary knowledge. Projects required in all classes.

MOUNTLAKE TERRACE HIGH SCHOOL IN MOUNTLAKE TERRACE, WASHINGTON

SCHOOL DEMOGRAPHICS

Mountlake Terrace High School is located in suburban Mountlake Terrace, about 20 minutes north of downtown Seattle. One of five high schools in the Edmonds School District, Mountlake Terrace opened in 1960. In 1991, it moved into a new facility with 50 classrooms, 2 art rooms, 2 music rooms, and an up-to-date theater and gym.

Mountlake Terrace offers a 9–12 program for 1,865 students, who are served by 83 teachers, 4 administrators, 6 counselors, a drug and alcohol counselor, 15 educational assistants, a career center specialist, a school-to-careers coordinator, and a library specialist. Thirteen percent of the students are on free and reduced lunch, and approximately one-fourth are Asian American, African American, and Hispanic. Some teachers claim that district personnel once perceived Terrace as a school "on the wrong side of the tracks." Transforming such impressions, Terrace has claimed center stage as a pioneering high school in Washington State.

WHY MI?

During the late 1980s, administrators at the school wondered whether MI-based teaching could motivate underachieving students. Then-Principal Elaine Klein and a few others at the school were also interested in applying for a Washington State Governor's grant. The two ideas of MI teaching and grant funding were fortuitously combined, and, in 1989, Mountlake Terrace High School received a prestigious Schools for the 21st Century Grant.

The purpose of the grant was, through schoolwide change, to become a model of education for the next century. The grant paid for 10 days of professional development time, provided supplemental funding of approximately $50,000 annually, and offered waivers from local bargaining agreements, district policies, and state rules. The grant also had another significant feature: a six-year time line. With the ideal mix of money, time, and freedom from restrictive regulations—along with the state board of education's mandate to "radically" restructure—Mountlake Terrace High School was poised for reinventing high school education.

CREATING AN MI PROGRAM

Beginning with the 1989–90 school year, grant moneys went to extensive MI-based professional development. The expectation was that each Mountlake Terrace teacher would use MI in classroom instruction. All teachers participated in one or more forms of MI professional development: working with consultants at the school, attending local conferences and workshops, or participating in a week-long MI Institute at Harvard University. Science teacher Dan Wilson says that as a result of these experiences "a new mind-set emerged." Teachers' beliefs about student ability began to change, and so did their ideas about teaching.

The next step was to move the MI ideas into instruction. Because little information existed about MI at the high school level, some Terrace staff decided to use one another as MI resources. They used released days to write MI lessons together. Such co-planning resulted in more hands-on, collaborative, and kinesthetic instruction than the former "stand and deliver" kind of teaching. For example, science teachers planned a cellular biology lesson that asked students to demonstrate 10 characteristics of living things without using words. The students initially struggled with their teachers' request, but soon enough they made charts, mobiles, puppets, songs, dramatic presentations, advertisements, and videos to demonstrate their learning.

In math, an emphasis was placed on teaching geometry and algebra kinesthetically. Teacher Eeva Reeder asked students to make angles with their bodies and then rotate around axes. They next learned about geometric shapes by building them and studied how to graph algebraic equations by "becoming them" on a giant x/y grid in the school courtyard. MI learning was occurring in many classrooms throughout the school.

Mountlake Terrace teachers discovered newfound quality and creativity in students' assignments. For a while, the staff excitedly told one another about the work being produced in their classrooms, but they realized that seeing would be better than telling. As a result, "Days of Celebration" were held to display and discuss students' assignments.

In addition to professional development and pedagogical changes, Mountlake Terrace took strides to restructure its total school program. Interested in Gardner's ideas about education for understanding, Terrace deemphasized chronologically sequenced courses and, instead, promoted three levels of disciplinary knowledge: entry, core, and application. The three-tier structure emphasized in-depth learning over seat time and age factors.

Initiated in 1991, this approach to curricular sequencing remains in place today. At the *entry* level, students are expected to develop basic skills in essential areas such as communications, math, science, and technology. The second or *core* level builds upon the basic skills by extending student knowledge in what would be considered the "traditional" curriculum of most high school programs. At the third or *application* level, students must prepare a final, public presentation of a self-directed project that exemplifies their individual talents, interests, and accomplishments.

In addition to revamping grade-level configurations, Mountlake Terrace teachers decided that students should demonstrate their disciplinary knowledge not only through paper-and-pencil means, but by applying it in real-world ways. Taking another dramatic step in high school restructuring in 1991, the school exchanged Carnegie units for competencies. To earn their high school diplomas, Mountlake Terrace students would have to demonstrate 16 core competencies. These competencies revolved around the multiple intelligences, with a special emphasis on the personal intelligences.

THE MI CURRICULUM

Supported by their administration, one another, and the School for the 21st Century Grant, Mountlake Terrace staff markedly changed their school's program. Many teachers adopted MI lesson planning. Project-based learning became mandatory, and students were required to apply their knowledge, rather than merely accrue seat time to earn a high school diploma. The competencies adopted in 1991 (shown in Figure 4.2) continue to drive the schoolwide program and individual classroom curriculum.

Some of the competencies in Figure 4.2 are evident in teacher Jay Kirk's core writing class. Kirk teaches writing skills by having his students write letters to several audiences: colleges, newspapers, and businesses. For example, they write to colleges about admissions requirements and businesses about employment possibilities. They also write articles for their school newspaper and send editorials to local newspapers. Through their letters, students practice the competencies of communicating with a variety of audiences, articulating their individual values, and applying critical thinking skills. An added plus for the students is the responses they receive from their letters, which often arrive within a week.

To prepare his students for their letter-writing assignments, Kirk teaches writing concepts through several intelligences. His students learn the structure of different letters through visuals, role-play the impact of their writing on others, analyze points of view and persuasive elements of song

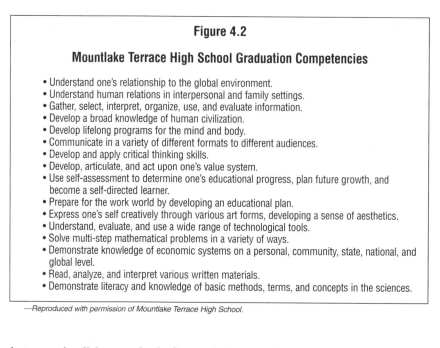

Figure 4.2

Mountlake Terrace High School Graduation Competencies

- Understand one's relationship to the global environment.
- Understand human relations in interpersonal and family settings.
- Gather, select, interpret, organize, use, and evaluate information.
- Develop a broad knowledge of human civilization.
- Develop lifelong programs for the mind and body.
- Communicate in a variety of different formats to different audiences.
- Develop and apply critical thinking skills.
- Develop, articulate, and act upon one's value system.
- Use self-assessment to determine one's educational progress, plan future growth, and become a self-directed learner.
- Prepare for the work world by developing an educational plan.
- Express one's self creatively through various art forms, developing a sense of aesthetics.
- Understand, evaluate, and use a wide range of technological tools.
- Solve multi-step mathematical problems in a variety of ways.
- Demonstrate knowledge of economic systems on a personal, community, state, national, and global level.
- Read, analyze, and interpret various written materials.
- Demonstrate literacy and knowledge of basic methods, terms, and concepts in the sciences.

—*Reproduced with permission of Mountlake Terrace High School.*

lyrics, and collaboratively draft sample letters before writing individually. In planning lessons, Kirk sometimes finds it helpful to use the MI instructional and assessment "menus" shown in Figure 4.3.

Noting that most productive human work occurs in the form of projects, Gardner recommends that students conduct school-based projects to acquire skills needed as adults. At Mountlake Terrace, students complete projects in many classes. Teachers identify the concepts, skills, and competencies to integrate into project work. They also guide students through the stages of project initiation, implementation, presentation, reflection, and assessment.

Inspired by MI implications for all students, Kate Cleavall, a special education teacher, redesigned her science course to include a yearlong project and to integrate her students' individualized educational plans. To successfully complete the class project, entitled Biology Through Caretaking, students must, in addition to other requirements, be responsible for the care and well-being of a plant or animal. Cleavall guides students through the various stages of project completion, as shown in Figure 4.4.

As described in the figure, this project includes research skills and essential science concepts such as change, cause and effect, structure and function, systems and interaction, and variation and diversity. It integrates

Figure 4.3

MI Instructional and Assessment Menus:
Sample Tasks Used in Writing Class at Mountlake Terrace High School

Linguistic Menu:
- Use storytelling to . . .
- Write a poem, myth, legend, short play, or news article about . . .
- Lead a class discussion on . . .
- Create a radio program about . . .
- Invent slogans for . . .
- Conduct an interview of . . . on . . .

Logical-Mathematical Menu:
- Create story problems for . . .
- Translate . . . into a formula . . .
- Create a time line of . . .
- Invent a strategy game that . . .
- Make up analogies to explain . . .
- Design a code for . . .

Kinesthetic Menu:
- Role-play or simulate . . .
- Choreograph a dance of . . .
- Invent a board or floor game of . . .
- Build or construct a . . .
- Devise a scavenger hunt to . . .
- Design a product for . . .

Visual Menu:
- Chart, map, cluster, or graph . . .
- Create a slide show, videotape, or photo album of . . .
- Design a poster, bulletin board, or mural of . . .
- Create advertisements for . . .
- Vary the size and shape of . . .
- Color code the process of . . .

Musical Menu:
- Give a presentation with musical accompaniment on . . .
- Sing a rap or song that explains . . .
- Indicate the rhythmical patterns in . . .
- Explain how a piece of music is similar to . . .
- Use music to enhance learning . . .
- Create a musical collage to depict . . .

Interpersonal Menu:
- Conduct a meeting to . . .
- Act out diverse perspectives on . . .
- Intentionally use . . . social skills to learn about . . .
- Teach someone else about . . .
- Collaboratively plan rules or procedures to . . .
- Give and receive feedback on . . .

Intrapersonal Menu:
- Set and pursue a goal to . . .
- Describe how you feel about . . .
- Describe your personal values about . . .
- Write a journal entry on . . .
- Do a project of your choice on . . .
- Self-assess your work in . . .

Naturalist Menu:
- Collect and categorize data . . .
- Keep a journal of observations about . . .
- Explain how a plant or animal species resembles . . .
- Make a taxonomy of . . .
- Specify the characteristics of . . .
- Attend an outdoor field trip to . . .

—Adapted from Campbell, L., Campbell, B., & Dickinson, D. (1999, 2nd ed., & 1996, 1st ed.). Teaching and learning through multiple intelligences. Needham Heights, MA: Allyn & Bacon. Reprinted by permission of publisher.

several of the school's graduation competencies and requires that students put their knowledge into real-world application. Creating such projects requires much thought and preparation on the teacher's part.

As Cleavall explains, "It takes a long time to develop an MI project, but when you do, you have something wonderful to teach." She has witnessed significant academic and motivational results from her efforts. For example,

Cleavall describes one of her success stories: "There was a student who skipped his probation meetings, didn't go home, didn't go to other classes, but never missed science. His mom would call to ask if we had seen him,

---

Figure 4.4

Biology Through Caretaking Project at Mountlake Terrace High School

Beginning the Project:
- Create a journal to track progress and to collect research information.
- Choose either a plant or animal to research, one that is capable of being sustained in the classroom. (Previous selections have included roses, cactuses, herbs, jade plants, protozoa, guinea pigs, crickets, snakes, fish, rats, mice, lizards, and tarantulas.)
- Research background information on the selected organism.
- Identify necessary supplies.
- Prepare a budget for approval.
- Create an environmentally correct cage or container.
- Acquire the organism and begin caretaking.

Expectations During the Year:
- Keep a daily journal that logs research, reflection, progress, problems, notes, and emotions, including perseverance and effort.
- Answer daily questions from class and explain how they apply to the organism.
- Maintain total responsibility for the organism and its well-being.
- Identify the variables that affect the organism's ecosystem.
- Keep the organism alive throughout the year.
- Seek outside expertise including online resources.
- Determine how your actions affect the organism.

Demonstrating Expertise During the Third Trimester:
- Demonstrate expertise in taking care of the organism.
- Write a formal, word-processed scientific study that persuades the audience of the study's value and demonstrates solid research processes and biological principles.
- Conduct and document the study with the organism.
- Reflect on your experiences, as described in the next section.
- Submit a completed journal.
- If the original organism or its offspring is alive and well, and all other requirements are met satisfactorily, you will earn an *A* grade.

Reflecting on Your Learning:
- Chronicle your learning throughout the project.
- Articulate what you learned about yourself as a learner.
- Review the project's progress.
- Reflect upon the degree of success of your work, and identify the key elements contributing to success.
- Identify what you would do differently next time.
- Identify what was satisfying about the experience.
- Acknowledge and celebrate success.

—*Reproduced with permission of Kate Cleavall and Mountlake Terrace High School.*

and we had, because he attended science every day to take care of his bird: a zebra finch. MI has tremendous application in special education, even though this hasn't been discussed much."

APPLICATION PROJECTS

Prepared by carrying out their classroom projects, Terrace students must complete a high-stakes *application project* in order to graduate. While open-ended in nature, these projects—completed over two trimesters—must reflect individual students' interests and fall within one of these categories: planning an event, learning a new skill, exploring a career, designing a product, offering a service, doing research, or conducting a special investigation. Students must receive mentoring from community experts, undertake some form of research, and give final presentations. Terrace students are aware of the importance of their application projects. If students do not complete the projects properly, they do not graduate. In this event, students begin the 24-week process all over again or seek high school equivalency certificates.

In the past, application projects have included home construction, video production, composition and performance of music, the writing of children's books, career explorations, or the design of web pages. In fact, some students added to Mountlake Terrace's website for part of their project work. The project's grade is based upon the written proposal, public speaking, product exhibition, bibliography, and a final reflective essay. Experts in the field who have mentored students during their projects help teachers and community volunteers assess the students' progress. They know in advance that experts will be evaluating their work, and most respond by creating high-quality projects and presentations. To successfully complete this long-term assignment, students have acquired the essential skills of time management, problem solving, record keeping, self-assessment, and effective communication. The application projects culminate Mountlake Terrace students' high school careers and simultaneously prepare them for their futures.

CURRICULAR OBSTACLES TO MI

The focus on improving instruction initiated by a grant over a decade ago continues to permeate Mountlake Terrace High School's culture. Many of the original staff members have moved on, new staff have arrived, but engaging teaching remains a top priority among staff, administrators, and the students, who have come to expect it. Nevertheless, schoolwide support for MI has weakened due to several factors.

In 1991, Mountlake Terrace moved into a new facility. Simultaneously, the school adopted a three-strand schedule because of a school district policy against using portables. To accommodate the burgeoning numbers of students, the school offered three staggered and mutually exclusive strands of seven-period days. Teacher Dan Wilson describes the impact of these changes on the staff: "The teachers no longer see everyone. The schedule is so fragmented that it prevents collegial dialogue. Still, over 50 percent of the teachers at the school use MI in their instruction. Teachers believe that kids' minds work in different ways and to optimize academic success they need to teach and assess them multimodally."

Wilson's math colleague, Eeva Reeder, identifies another common challenge to MI instruction: "Even if we are informed, we can't always act on our beliefs because of 50-minute class periods, college entrance requirements, standardized tests, and the demands of state standards. With the quantity of information to convey and our limited time, lecturing seems the most efficient approach. Once you know about MI, though, you can't ignore it. As a teacher, I am morally obligated to act on my understanding of human intelligence. MI makes learning more accessible in my classroom."

Many teachers at Mountlake Terrace respond to the moral challenge Reeder has identified. She explains, "Students expect diverse modes of delivery from their teachers. In fact, some ask questions like, 'Can I draw this out?' 'I work well in groups. Can we break into small groups for this assignment?' "

Dan Wilson concurs, "Students are more involved in their assignments and have more pride in their work. We expect them to find ways to represent their knowledge with high-quality work. Because they have choices to express themselves individually, we expect more quality."

CLASSROOM ASSESSMENT AND ACADEMIC ACHIEVEMENT

Before Mountlake Terrace High School explored multiple intelligences, assessment primarily consisted of paper-and-pencil tests. Today, while teachers still use traditional measures when appropriate to determine progress in individual classes, performance-based measures predominate. Biology teacher Dan Wilson explains that with MI instruction and assessment, "we look for a variety of ways kids can express what they have learned. The options empower them. We as teachers realized, though, that our criteria had to be clear enough so that kids could understand and visualize the assignments from their areas of strength."

The teachers responded to this challenge by using rubrics and scoring guides that specify their expectations. Additionally, project-based assessment now dominates in each classroom: presentations, exhibitions, demonstrations, models, and visual representations of learning. For example, when the teacher asked students to assess a lesson in biology, students had to devise a way to teach the structure and parts of a cell to someone who knew nothing about the topic. Student responses included a videotape, a play, a song, and a guided tour of the classroom turned into a cell.

Courses at Mountlake Terrace receive *A, B, C, I,* and *NC* grades. An *I* indicates that course work is incomplete and the student may have additional time to complete the credit. An *NC* grade indicates the student will not receive credit and must retake the class. Students must earn a *C* or better in every class to be considered competent. If students feel they can demonstrate the desired outcomes without taking the class, they may challenge it and move to more demanding course work. Believing that there are always more than minimum requirements to be met, students may pursue honors-level work for most classes by completing additional requirements. For successful achievement of these tasks, students receive an honors (H) designation on their transcripts.

Teachers at Mountlake Terrace have broadened the responsibility for assessment to include people from outside the classroom. As noted earlier, students' mentors help teachers assess their application projects. In many cases, business people, government employees, college professors, parents, and other students also attend application project presentations, and all may provide formal or informal feedback.

Students rise to the challenge of being assessed by knowledgeable, real-world experts. There are other benefits as well. When peers observe an outstanding exhibition, they are inspired to attain similar standards themselves. Likewise, when teachers observe their students perform, they know with certainty that students excel at something and that they can use their knowledge in meaningful, important ways.

DISTRICT, STATE, AND STANDARDIZED TEST ACHIEVEMENT

In addition to classroom assessment, Mountlake Terrace High School students take district- and state-mandated tests as well as national standardized tests. The school performs the same as or better than its district and state counterparts.

The Edmonds School District Writing Assessment, developed by district teachers, is administered to 10th graders annually. Students write on one of two possible topics; raters evaluate their papers according to four traits—content, sentences, voice, and conventions—on a 1–5 scale (1 is low, 5 is high). Eighty-three percent of Mountlake Terrace 10th graders score at 2.5 or above, which is comparable to district averages.

The Curriculum Framework Aptitude System (CFAS) is a state-mandated standardized achievement test administered to all juniors. The test has no national norm but, instead, ranks students against state norms in English, math, social studies, and science. Mountlake Terrace's scores have consistently risen, moving from below district averages to above district averages. Students outperform their statewide peers in English, social studies, and math. In fact, they score 10 percentage points above the state norm in math and score the highest of the five high schools in their district.

On the national standardized Scholastic Aptitude Test, Mountlake Terrace students have consistently improved their scores. Between 1994 and 1996, SAT verbal scores rose from 430 to 501. During the same three years, SAT math scores rose from 477 to 519. As on the state CFAS test, students outperform their state and national peers in math achievement.

Another perspective on students' math scores appeared in the large daily newspaper, *The Seattle Times's* 1997–1998 School Guide. The *Times* analyzed five years' worth of math test scores from all public high schools in Washington State. Only nine high schools in the state had pronounced upward trends in student performance on math tests. One of the nine schools was Mountlake Terrace High School.

Mountlake Terrace High School has received other forms of acknowledgment:

- The student newspaper, *The Hawkeye,* placed first in the nation among high school newspapers and won the national Pacemaker award, considered to be the Pulitzer Prize in scholastic journalism.
- The Debate Club has won 65 awards and sent members to state and national competitions.
- The Jazz Ensemble won first place at the Lionel Hampton Jazz Festival and the Viking Jazz Festival.
- The school's math team has placed in state and regional competitions.
- The technology program was selected as the Technology Education Program of the year in 1998 by the Washington Technology Education Association.
- *Redbook* magazine identified the school as Washington State's representative in the "America's Best High School" program in 1996.

- In addition to numerous national, regional, and state awards, the school's former principal, Elaine Klein, who originally sparked interest in MI at the school, received a Washington State Award for Excellence in Education.

Visitors to Mountlake Terrace High School may initially be impressed with the features of a large, contemporary physical facility. The perceptive observer, however, will soon realize that it is the broad range of instructional strategies and assessment tools that make Mountlake Terrace what it set out to be 10 years ago, a school for the 21st century. MI provided the infrastructure that has enabled Terrace to accomplish this mission.

LINCOLN HIGH SCHOOL IN STOCKTON, CALIFORNIA

SCHOOL DEMOGRAPHICS

Lincoln High School is one of three high schools in the Lincoln Unified School District in suburban Stockton, California. More than half of the school's 2,600 students are ethnically diverse, 26 percent receive aid for dependent children, and 13 percent are limited-English-proficient students. The school employs 122 teachers, whose classes include approximately 35 students each. The school has a chief executive officer, 2 principals, 4 deans, 4 counselors, 4 counselor associates, and 10 aides. Lincoln's program spans grades 9–12 and includes ESL, gifted and talented, and other offerings to meet students' special needs. The school is well known for its strong visual and performing arts program, which enrolls more than 900 students in its courses. Daily attendance at Lincoln is 97 percent.

WHY MI?

In the spring of 1990, Lincoln administrators and staff applied for a state planning grant. They had two key reasons for wanting to restructure the entire school. First, Lincoln's population had changed dramatically since the school's founding in 1954. Initially, the school served an affluent, white, and middle- to upper-middle-class community. By 1990, Lincoln students mirrored the demographics of the city of Stockton, with increased ethnic, socioeconomic, and language diversity. Sixteen different languages and cultures were represented in the student population. Twenty percent of the students were Asian, another 20 percent were Hispanic, and 11 percent were

African American. The teachers wanted to ensure equal access to rich and appropriate educational experiences for all students.

While applying for the California Plan-to-Plan grant, the administrators and teachers engaged in honest, extensive dialogue about teaching and learning. When asked to identify their most memorable learning experiences, teachers acknowledged that they had few. They assumed the same was true for their students. A critical question arose: "How might we change our teaching to make learning memorable and powerful for students?" Answering this question was the second motivator for schoolwide change.

Some teachers and administrators suggested that MI theory might provide theoretical support for instructional change. Those familiar with MI shared information about the theory with the rest of the Lincoln staff in a professional development program. With grant money and a theoretical ally, Lincoln High School started down the rocky road of educational reform.

CREATING AN MI PROGRAM

Teachers' curiosity about MI was peaked by the initial presentation, so the school launched a variety of other professional development experiences. Some teachers visited other schools. Nearly all attended a series of inservice days with MI consultants. In addition, eight focus groups were established at the school to research MI theory and its curricular implications. Entire school days were dedicated to reporting back findings to the whole staff. Teachers' innovative ideas were met with consistent support from site and district administrators. According to science teacher Pam Martin, "We are guaranteed support to be risk-takers, and this has allowed us to work with MI. The administration has practiced what it preaches even at the highest levels."

While teachers were engaging in extensive professional development, so too were the parents. Another component of the Plan-to-Plan grant was to invite stakeholders to participate in the school. Parents and community members learned about MI at back-to-school workshops. Coffee meetings were held in parents' homes, and a local museum hosted a communitywide discussion featuring MI consultants, architects, artists, and current and former students. Lincoln's parents grew supportive of curricular changes with one significant exception.

Although Lincoln made every effort to inform the parents of its current students about MI, school staff overlooked the future parent population, those with their children in feeder middle schools. After learning of Lincoln's intent to radically alter its curriculum, some parents grew concerned. As a teacher explained, this "put the brakes on" the school's fast-paced restructuring efforts. Such parental doubts also increased some staff members' resistance to the proposed curricular changes and unleashed dissension at the school.

Another blow to the initial enthusiasm came in 1991, when Lincoln did not receive the state implementation grant that was to follow the Plan-to-Plan grant. Without the second grant, Lincoln could not fund its proposed curricular changes. This disappointing news, coupled with the discord among staff and parents, forced a schoolwide reexamination of the restructuring process. Slowly, a climate emerged that permitted teachers to move in directions comfortable for each individual teacher. One direction that was comfortable for many was MI-based instruction.

Teachers began altering instruction in their individual classrooms and collectively in teams. New interdisciplinary, team-teaching efforts evolved, and site- and district-level administrators supported those who attempted to teach in ways "that matched how students learned." In fact, as one of Lincoln's two principals Louise King explains, "Giving students information in different ways and encouraging them to present their learning in different ways is valued districtwide. Variety and choice are important for all students."

MI CURRICULUM AND INSTRUCTION

English teacher Chris Morgan explains how MI changed teaching at Lincoln High School. In considering her own teaching, Morgan reflects, "When I used to teach *Romeo and Juliet*, the students were bored. Now we go out in the hall and draw scenes on butcher paper, then make props, add music, and act the play out. Teachers spend money on things like crayons, paint, and butcher paper for high school kids. This was unheard of before."

The changes Morgan has made in her teaching are evident throughout the school. Principal Norrie Bean adds, "Before MI, instruction consisted of lectures, textbooks, and worksheets. Now that's minimal schoolwide. At least 50 percent of the time students are doing group work and projects. Students do projects in every single class."

Samples of enriched, MI-based instruction are evident in most departments throughout the school. For example, in a junior math class, students tackle the real-world mathematics of oil spills, bees' honeycombs, population growth, and the best sizes and shapes for fencing an area. To do so, they use a variety of tools, make graphs, hold group consultations, and give individual and group presentations. Students are using the math of engineers and scientists.

In a 9th grade literature class, students select books to read, conduct literary discussions, make visuals of their readings, do role-plays, reflect on their literacy experiences outside the classroom, and do self-assessments. In world history, students create semantic maps of historical time periods and learn artistic techniques to augment their linguistic content. In science, they write and illustrate myths, using elements of the periodic table as characters. When studying cells, student construct models or create visual metaphors of cell structures. For example, one student made the following analogies in her drawing of a cell: cardboard served as the cell wall, netlike material represented the cell membrane, recycled paper bags symbolized cytoplasm, a ball of string stood for the nucleolus, and a battery for the mitochondria. Teaching to "intellectual diversity," as science teacher Pam Martin describes MI instruction, has become embedded in school policies, documents, and beliefs. "The mission of Lincoln High School, as a mutually supportive member of the community," the school's statement reads,

> is to prepare each student to be a multi-skilled, well-rounded, responsible learner, who, by way of his or her uniqueness and response to the education provided here, will productively contribute to our global community.

To emphasize this mission, the school articulates its core beliefs, for example, "Students and teachers have multiple intelligences"—and the school "pledges" to offer academic programs that engage the multiple intelligences. Principal Louise King explains, "Helping students learn in a variety of ways is part of the belief system and culture at Lincoln High School."

As a large suburban high school, Lincoln offers a comprehensive academic program with 12 departments or programs. These include business and applied arts, English, foreign language, multilingual programs, math, science, social science, physical education, special education, non-departmental programs, and visual and performing arts, which enroll more than 900 students. An additional and unique program at Lincoln is called Integrated Studies.

INTEGRATED STUDIES PROGRAMS

Lincoln's daily schedule is made up of 55-minute classes, but several interdisciplinary programs are scheduled with back-to-back class periods. Known as *integrated studies*, these courses are team-taught and blend two or three disciplines thematically. Teachers emphasize the connections between the subjects while teaching core content for each. For example, in Integrated Studies 9/10, students take a three-hour block class that awards one credit each in language arts, science, and social studies. The theme of the course is "Understanding Our Personal, Social, and Physical Worlds." In integrated studies courses, students typically conduct long-term research inquiries. All such courses are considered college-preparatory and include students of all ability levels, even special education and gifted students.

For the 1998–1999 and 1999–2000 years, Lincoln High School offered five integrated studies programs, as shown in Figure 4.5. The first of such integrated studies programs evolved from the school's Plan-to-Plan grant and

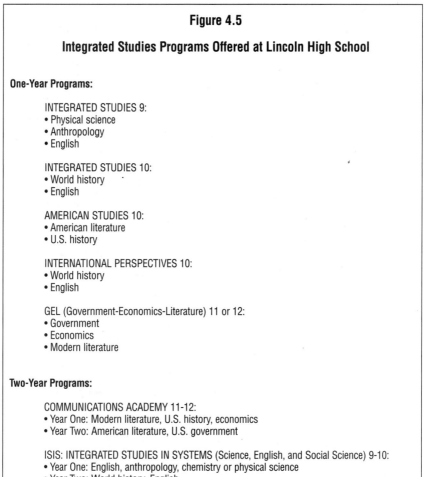

Figure 4.5

Integrated Studies Programs Offered at Lincoln High School

One-Year Programs:

INTEGRATED STUDIES 9:
• Physical science
• Anthropology
• English

INTEGRATED STUDIES 10:
• World history
• English

AMERICAN STUDIES 10:
• American literature
• U.S. history

INTERNATIONAL PERSPECTIVES 10:
• World history
• English

GEL (Government-Economics-Literature) 11 or 12:
• Government
• Economics
• Modern literature

Two-Year Programs:

COMMUNICATIONS ACADEMY 11-12:
• Year One: Modern literature, U.S. history, economics
• Year Two: American literature, U.S. government

ISIS: INTEGRATED STUDIES IN SYSTEMS (Science, English, and Social Science) 9-10:
• Year One: English, anthropology, chemistry or physical science
• Year Two: World history, English

—*Reproduced with permission of Lincoln High School.*

is called Integrated Studies in Systems (ISIS). ISIS is an interdisciplinary, project-based program that combines science, social science, and English credits into a three-period block for 9th and 10th grade students. It is an inclusive program open to all students, including those with special needs.

Three teachers work with 90 students for two years to forge a collaborative, personalized learning environment. In ISIS, students are asked to think critically about texts, to conceptualize connections among subject areas, and to pursue personal research inquiries. For example, during one quarter, students address "What is diversity?" In biology, they explore the source of organic diversity and variation in DNA. They learn the tools and processes of the scientist by using microscopes, making slides, and using micro pipettes. In English, they study *Romeo and Juliet* and learn to analyze language, cultural conflict, and the difficulty many face in accepting diversity. And, in world history, students examine diversity in cultural, political, and natural systems.

Because ISIS spans three class periods, teachers use the time flexibly. Some days, all three periods will be dedicated to one subject. For example, one day in first period, small groups of students studied aspects of enzymes and planned brief presentations to teach their content to class members. During second period, they gave their brief presentations on diffusion, adhesion and cohesion, glycerols and fatty acids, DNA and RNA. During third period, students were quizzed on the information from all presentations.

According to the ISIS course descriptions, whatever students study, and however their class time may be structured, "the multiple intelligences are incorporated into all activities and projects." ISIS teachers feel that their program enhances their own intellectual development as well. English teacher Chris Morgan says that "MI develops our intelligences as teachers. We become more metacognitive about our own processes and learn and grow from the strengths of everyone in our team."

As in the other five MI school programs described in this book, student projects are an important part of learning at Lincoln High School in general and the ISIS program in particular. Each semester ISIS students ask questions about their world and conduct inquiries in search of answers. The projects integrate social science perspectives, scientific issues, and literary selections, as evident in the outline in Figure 4.6 Once students have identified answers to their questions, they become responsible for taking community action by informing or influencing others.

Figure 4.6

Lincoln High School's ISIS Inquiry Outline

A Guide to Creating an ISIS Inquiry Outline

(**You** Create Your <u>Own</u> Outline)*

Essential Question:
How does an ISIS student create an authentic, important, and thorough research-based inquiry?

I. Introduction
  A. What is the Essential Question and the environmental impact to my topic?
  (Environment: the social, cultural, scientific/technological, and natural world)
  What are the social, cultural, scientific/technological, and natural interconnections involved?
  (NETWORKS)

  B. Why did I choose this topic? What is interesting about this topic?

  C. Beyond my own personal interest, why is the local and global impact of this topic important now and for the future? (BOUNDARIES)

II. Research Methodology
  A. Where did I find my information (People, Places, Links)?

  B. What are the major sources that informed my research?

III. Social Science Perspectives
  A. How does the historical perspective of my topic help me understand the answer to my essential question? Who are significant people connected to my topic? How does my time line help illustrate the evolutionary nature of my topic? (DEVELOPMENT)

  B. How has human involvement related to my topic created an environmental problem over time? (CYCLES)

  C. What is the current environmental issue related to my topic?

  D. How does my interview help me gain perspective on my topic? (Include quotes.)

  E. What is the historical, scientific, and technological background involved?

IV. Scientific Connections
  A. What was my controlled experiment? (Make references to data and journal findings.)

  B. How do my research conclusions inform the answer(s) to my essential question? (FLOW-THROUGH)

  C. What are my research hypotheses?

  D. What suggestions do I have for further research (hypotheses, experimental designs)?

V. Literary Experience
  A. What literature (fiction/nonfiction) have I read that informs my topic? (Include and justify supportive quotations.)

  B. How does this literature help me understand the answer to my essential question?

  OR

  A. How does my literary creation powerfully express my knowledge of this topic? (Include selections from your work.)

  B. How does my literary creation help me answer or gain perspective on my essential question?

(Continued on next page)

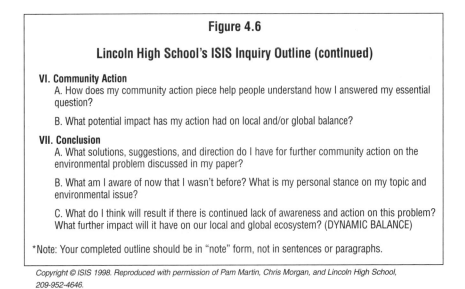

Figure 4.6

Lincoln High School's ISIS Inquiry Outline (continued)

VI. Community Action
  A. How does my community action piece help people understand how I answered my essential question?

  B. What potential impact has my action had on local and/or global balance?

VII. Conclusion
  A. What solutions, suggestions, and direction do I have for further community action on the environmental problem discussed in my paper?

  B. What am I aware of now that I wasn't before? What is my personal stance on my topic and environmental issue?

  C. What do I think will result if there is continued lack of awareness and action on this problem? What further impact will it have on our local and global ecosystem? (DYNAMIC BALANCE)

*Note: Your completed outline should be in "note" form, not in sentences or paragraphs.

ISIS INQUIRY OUTLINE

Once each semester, ISIS students present exhibitions of their projects to parents and community members. Because students remain in the program for two years, they compile a record of their research questions and the intelligences they used in their work. Twice annually students reflect on their interests and intelligence strengths using the record shown in Figure 4.7.

By reviewing these records, students are encouraged to take risks. As one ISIS student reflected, "During 9th grade, I wrote an essay about my project and included a picture of myself. Now I have learned so many more ways to present information. For example, I would use music that related to my topic, lots of visuals, and do things to interact with my audience. I have learned a lot about communicating."

Teacher Pam Martin identifies another benefit of ISIS participation: "Students are encouraged to take greater academic risks after being in ISIS. They go on to AP English and AP science when they would not have otherwise done so."

The success of the ISIS program has spawned other integrated study offerings at the school. After ISIS was created in 1991, many Lincoln students requested, and received, similar programs during their junior and senior high school years.

COMMUNICATIONS ACADEMY

Can you imagine hundreds of high school students flocking to poetry readings or, better yet, writing the poetry to be read? Such events occur once quarterly at Lincoln High. The Poet's Café is located in a former office building close to the high school campus. The Café is a project of the Communications Academy. Academy students have total responsibility for running the Café as a business. They organize the monthly readings, the food to be served, the Café's budget, the bookkeeping, and the community advertising.

The Café is open one evening per month for teachers, students, parents, and other community members. Hundreds of students attend the readings for a variety of reasons. In addition to the fact that the Café is enjoyable for young and old alike, students receive credit for English assignments by writing and reading poetry or other literary works, as well as social sciences assignment credit if their writing addresses a topic of study such as the Bill of Rights.

Sherry Pratt, the teacher who organizes the Poet's Café, once taught with the ISIS team. As Norrie Bean, principal of Lincoln, explains, "As a result of

---

Figure 4.7

Lincoln High School's ISIS Exhibition, Community Action, and Multiple Intelligences Record

NAME _____

Essential Question:
What MI strategies will you use in your Exhibition?
What will your Community Action Product be?
What MI strategies will you use in your Community Action Product?

—Reproduced with permission of Lincoln High School.

the Integrated Studies programs during their first two years in high school, some students become persuasive advocates about their education and pressure the administration into providing more opportunities for integrated studies. The Communication Academy is one example of their advocacy."

The Communications Academy is a two-year program for juniors and seniors. During the junior year, students earn three credits in modern literature, U.S. history, and economics. The senior year focuses on American literature and U.S. government. A sample, month-long assignment from the fall 1998 quarter is shown in Figure 4.8.

CLASSROOM ASSESSMENT AND ACADEMIC ACHIEVEMENT

Principal Norrie Bean describes classroom assessment before MI, "Students were asked to memorize content, and then they were tested." Teacher Pam Martin describes current practices, "Since MI, teachers are assessing projects, art work, videotapes, and presentations. Group assessment is now common. There is also more self-assessment."

Part of students' self-assessment often includes examining their interaction with school work. For example, after students performed scenes from *Romeo and Juliet*, teacher Chris Morgan asked them, "What did you do that helped you understand the play better?" Student responses included:

- "Through role-playing, we felt what the play meant."
- "I understand how much pressure Juliet felt."
- "Acting the play out made it seem real."
- "I found a side of myself and others that I didn't know was there."

Just as students reflect on their processes of understanding, Lincoln teachers continually appraise their instruction and assessment. The school district's tradition of decentralized management and teacher-driven curriculum contributes to an emphasis on teacher-determined pedagogical change. Janet Petsche, director of student services for Lincoln Unified School District, explains how some teachers react to state-required testing, "The district stated a few years ago that mandated tests will not dictate our programs. Instead, some teachers use test data to suggest ways to change instruction and assessment."

Principal Louise King explains that at Lincoln High School, they "are attempting to develop comprehensive assessment methods that inform instruction. We realize that there is not just one way to test and that by using multiple means we can discern the different talents of students, enhancing

Figure 4.8

Integrated Studies Assignment from Lincoln High School's Communications Academy Unit

Theme: Liberty, Justice, and Equality for All Americans—Protections Guaranteed by the Bill of Rights. Each group will investigate a specific amendment and create a video and a teaching session by doing the following activities:

1. Research information from numerous sources, including the Internet. Keep an individual process journal of all information gathered. Discuss in your group the importance of the amendment and how it protects individual rights.

2. Each person must write a reflective essay on the specified amendment. Identify the main provisions of the amendment, and connect these to your life. Why is this amendment considered important? What is valued and protected by this amendment? Why would this be important in your life? What controversies and problems exist? Submit your rough draft and final essay, typed in double-spaced 12-point font.

3. As a group, develop a video that will visually capture the heart and soul of your amendment. The video should include:

- A specific purpose and tone
- Storyboards
- Opening and closing credits
- Correct spelling and grammar
- Voice over
- Music that supports the purpose and tone
- Secondary textual imagery (optional)
- Special effects (optional) that support the purpose and tone

4. Prepare and conduct a teaching session that demonstrates an understanding of the amendment, its importance and relevance to the American people and our individual lives. Each person in the group must help prepare and present the teaching session; minimal requirements include:

- A short handout and visual for each person in the class
- An engaging demonstration of the amendment in actual practice
- Evidence that the rest of the class understands the importance of this amendment in their lives

5. Justify in your individual process journal what you and your group accomplish daily.

6. Read, discuss, and maintain a reading log of *Storming Heaven* by Denise Giardina.

7. Do self and group evaluations at the end of the unit.

Individual student responsibilities that will be assessed by the teacher and student:

- Individual process journal
- Individual contribution to video development process
- Video product
- Teaching session preparation and contribution
- Reading log
- Reflective essay
- Weekly participation
- Attendance at and/or preparation for the Poet's Café
- Self and group evaluations

—Reproduced with permission of Lincoln High School.

their strengths and improving their weaknesses. We truly value differences in the way people think."

As Pam Martin explains, the teachers at Lincoln enjoy "academic freedom." Without "teaching to the test," some teachers find value in adapting the new state assessment measures into instruction. English teacher Chris Morgan explains that one state assessment, the Learning Record Assessment System, "has actually helped us value MI teaching, because it requires multiple forms of assessment." The lesson teachers at Lincoln have learned is that using MI in careful and thoughtful tandem with new standards and state tests can increase learning and scores.

CALIFORNIA STATE'S LEARNING RECORD ASSESSMENT SYSTEM

The Learning Record Assessment System is an open record of literacy achievement used throughout California and across the United States. Teachers, parents, and students evaluate students' reading and writing skills using explicit performance standards. In addition to tracking the students' reading of textbooks and their writing class-required assignments, the Learning Record also logs what students read and write outside of school, teacher observations of classroom literacy behaviors, student and parent interviews, classroom role-plays, reader response logs, graphic organizers, videos and film reflections, oral readings, writing samples, and the connection of reading with students' life experiences. The reading and writing assessment criteria of the Learning Record are no mystery to Lincoln students. They are given the scales so that they can understand themselves as readers and writers. They are also responsible for setting individual goals based on the performance indicators and taking the necessary steps to achieve them. For example, students use the reading scale shown in Figure 4.9 to identify current and future skills

During the last quarter of the school year, students determine their placement on Reading Scale 3 for 9th–12th graders. With evidence from the Learning Record, they write a letter to their parents and teacher that justifies their placement. After this self-assessment, students determine their goals for the next school year. The teacher proceeds similarly. Based upon evidence in the Learning Record, the teacher identifies the performance level of each student and may adjust some placements accordingly. Students take their Learning Records home for parental review and response. Then, the returned documents are given to the next year's language arts teacher, who uses them to establish individualized goals at the outset of the new school year.

CALIFORNIA HIGH SCHOOL QUALITY INDICATORS

As in many states around the country, California is making significant changes in its mandated statewide testing of K–12 student achievement. Minimum competency tests for graduation have been and continue to be administered to Lincoln High School students, yet these are being revised. Standardized statewide testing did not take place from 1995–97 until the Stanford Test of Academic Skills, Fourth Edition, was available. During the 1997–98 school year all 9th, 10th, and 11th graders were tested in reading, language, mathematics, science, and social studies. At all three grade levels and in all five subjects, Lincoln students scored at or above average. According to Principal Louise King, "Lincoln's performance is not markedly better than other schools but slightly better." Her colleague, Norrie Bean, elucidates: "Our students rank at about the 55th percentile nationally, but in our county, we are the highest scoring school in most subjects."

Since the data from the 1997–98 tests served to create a school baseline, any longitudinal perspective of achievement is not yet available. Lincoln, however, has established the goal of exceeding the state's requirements for academic achievement. Principal Norrie Bean asserts that the "leadership team has a vision of continually restructuring the school and moving more and more toward MI. We will become even more creative."

Aside from test scores, there are other indicators of student success at Lincoln High School. In a California Department of Education High School Performance Report for the 1996–97 school year, Lincoln students ranked first in their district and second in their county in high school graduation rates. Further, while the state graduation rate is 87 percent, at Lincoln High School, it is over 97 percent. Additional comparative data from the California Department of Education High School Performance Report show that Lincoln students outscore district and statewide peers on SAT and ACT tests, more are enrolled in advanced placement courses, and more go on to attend college. In spite of these indicators, one teacher at Lincoln notes ironically, "A few staff members continue to resist MI instruction because of the old argument that kids won't get into college unless they are taught traditionally." The fact is that 90 percent of Lincoln graduates go on to attend two- or four-year colleges.

TEACHERS' AND STUDENTS' PERCEPTIONS CHANGE

Lincoln High School teachers value the contributions MI has made to their pedagogy. In addition, they appreciate the enhanced perceptions they have of themselves and their students. MI makes science teacher Pam Martin

Figure 4.9

Learning Record Reading Scale 3 for Grades 9–12: Becoming Accomplished in Reading

1
Ready for Accomplishment

Able to derive meaning from a variety of texts. Usually inexperienced in (a) challenging the writer's claims, evidence, or ideas, or (b) critiquing a text for style, logic, organization, etc. Expects texts to yield single interpretations. Sees most text as unrelated to life outside of school. May express frustration with density of course texts. Frequently abandons the reading of books, even those he or she has ostensibly chosen. Strategies include the use of some non-print media to collect information and a reliance on others for interpretations of text. Lacks familiarity with common text organizers, e.g., headings, index. May define himself or herself as one who does not read.

2
Somewhat Accomplished

Can read assigned course texts with preparation and support of visual, kinesthetic, and/or auditory supplement, e.g., graphics, enactment, listening for oral readings. Usually reads to fulfill assignments or for purposes outside of school rather than for pleasure. Strategies for getting course information include media other than text, e.g., collaborative groups and film or tapes; collaboration with peers to construct meaning in text; and conscious use of advance organizers and genre schemas. Can apply prior experience to some aspects of stories, biographies, and/or current events but may be unable to relate his or her own experience to more abstract ideas in course text.

3
Moderately Accomplished

Has some favorite kinds of reading. With preparation and support, can read aloud expressively from course texts. Knows the characteristics of a few genre. May rely on only a few strategies to construct meaning but shows a willingness to persist with some difficult texts. Makes associations between textual and personal experience. Can explain the way some texts are organized to help the reader derive meaning. Becoming aware, in interpreting texts, of the influence of their contexts, e.g., time period, subject matter, gender/status of author. Learning to share text interpretation with others. Developing skill in using course texts and outside reading as resources in class discussions and assignments.

4
Accomplished

Acknowledges the potential of texts to provoke multiple valid interpretations. Uses print conventions (punctuation, headings, index) to construct meaning in text. Assesses himself or herself as an effective reader of particular genres and can provide convincing evidence of same. Has strategies for unlocking difficult text. Able to evaluate information from multiple sources, e.g., texts and personal experiences. Able to acknowledge contradictory interpretations of text and previously held misconceptions about issues raised in class. Brings outside reading to bear on course work. Selects books for pleasure reading and for use in problem solving. Can manage the reading of long texts outside of class.

5
Exceptionally Accomplished

Reads avidly. Travels back and forth easily across the continuum of reading purposes: from reading for information to reading to enhance personal experience. Can discuss text interpretations tentatively, ready to modify and/or deepen initial impressions. Can elaborate on connections he or she is making with text and present convincing reasons as to what the connections add to personal understanding. Is able to weigh and compare relative strength and weakness, style, structure, credibility, or aesthetics of given and self-selected texts. Can explain, orally and/or in writing, the significance of the social, cultural, or political history of a text. Reads aloud fluently, with appropriate expression.

—Published as a component of the Learning Record Assessment System, copyright © Center for Language in Learning, 10610 Quail Canyon Rd., El Cajon, CA 92021. 619-443-6320. E-mail: lrecord@cll.org. See Barr & Syverson (1999).

continually remind herself that "kids are different and express themselves in different ways. It is necessary to teach in a variety of ways and use a variety of resources."

As a result of MI, says Communications Academy teacher Sherry Pratt, "there are more dynamic learning experiences in the classroom."

And, according to Principal Norrie Bean, "MI raises teachers' expectations and standards because students are expected to perform and to actively demonstrate their learning. Teachers also have a greater understanding of intellectual strengths, allowing for more student leadership. Teachers no longer accept that any student has an inability to learn!"

Pam Martin concurs, "Many of us have come to see students as capable of much more than we did previously. We also appreciate students who are not initially strong in logical-mathematical and linguistic intelligences. We expect everyone to shine in different areas."

Students respond to their teachers' enhanced perceptions by seeing school as a place for positive learning experiences. Principal Norrie Bean says MI "improves students' self-esteem and increases their connection to school." Perhaps this is one reason why more than 97 percent of Lincoln students attend school on a daily basis.

English teacher Chris Morgan adds, "MI makes school a safer place for kids, safer in a risk-taking way because students know they are appreciated. They notice everyone's strengths, and they become participants rather than vicarious players in their education. Students perceive themselves as multifaceted human beings because of MI."

Teachers are also encouraged to take more risks because of MI. Sherry Pratt says that "it gives students and teachers, all of us, chances to be acknowledged for our strengths. Confidence is boosted, and this encourages us to develop in other areas too."

Colleague Chris Morgan sums up many Lincoln teachers' and students' attitudes with the comment, "MI is a gift at the high school level."

LESSONS LEARNED FROM MI SCHOOL PROGRAMS 5

In this chapter we look at what kinds of schools value MI and why, positive effects for students (not just achievement gains), and insights gained from our work with the six schools. We also identify guiding principles that appear essential for any successful MI school endeavor.

WHAT KINDS OF SCHOOLS FIND VALUE IN MI?

What kinds of schools find value in MI? The six public schools featured in this book: Russell Elementary School in Lexington Kentucky; Expo for Excellence Elementary Magnet School in St. Paul, Minnesota; The Key Learning Community in Indianapolis, Indiana; Skyview Junior High School in Bothell, Washington; Lincoln High School in Stockton, California; and Mountlake Terrace High School in Mountlake Terrace, Washington, exhibit contrasting demographic features. Of the six, three, Russell, EXPO, and Key, are inner-city schools and three, Lincoln, Skyview, and Mountlake Terrace, are suburban. Two schools are small with approximately 200 students, and four range in size from 700 to 2,600.

There is racial, socioeconomic, and language diversity among the sites. Four schools serve student groups with 50 percent or more racial diversity, and two serve predominantly white students. Percentages of minority students range from 10 to 65 percent at the six schools. The number of students receiving free and reduced lunch varies from a low of 10 percent at one site to a high of 94 percent at another. Some schools have few limited-English-proficient students; 35 percent of the students at another speak English as a second language. Three—EXPO Elementary, the Key Learning Community, and Skyview Junior High School—were founded as MI programs. Three—Russell Elementary, Mountlake Terrace High School, and Lincoln High School—developed MI programs over time.

As evident in these demographics, MI's appeal is broad and inclusive whether a school is large or small, rich or poor, inner-city or suburban.

WHAT IS APPEALING ABOUT MI?

Why did schools with such varying demographics and needs all look to MI? Two primary motivations emerge. The schools founded as MI programs appeared to have different rationales than the three that evolved into MI sites. "Founding" schools were attracted to Gardner's theory for philosophic or theoretical reasons, whereas "developing" schools expressed pragmatic desires to enhance student achievement. While all six sites have realized the same ends, with improved student test scores, faculty morale, and student enthusiasm, they nevertheless adopted MI for different reasons.

The three schools that opened as MI sites—EXPO Elementary School, the Key Learning Community, and Skyview Junior High School—all had founding staff members who were intrigued by new research and wanted to answer core educational questions. At EXPO, administrators and teachers imagined a state-of-the-art, cognitive sciences research and theory-based program. They also wondered whether they could transform the concept of gifted education by claiming that every child was gifted. Similarly, at Key Learning Community, teachers and administrators were philosophically opposed to the notion of remedial education and wanted to craft a program that identified and built upon the strengths of every child. At Skyview Junior High, founding staff members viewed MI as capable of responding to their core question: "How can we best meet the needs of the adolescent?"

The "developing" schools—Russell Elementary School, Mountlake Terrace High School, and Lincoln High School—were primarily motivated to adopt MI due to concerns for lagging student achievement. At Russell Elementary School, a new administrator had a single, initial goal of improving student achievement. Russell students historically had scored below district and county peers on standardized tests. At Mountlake Terrace High School, administrators and teachers felt confident that MI-based instruction would motivate underachieving students. At Lincoln High School, teachers were concerned that traditional secondary instruction was a mismatch for their rapidly changing student population. The teachers hoped that student achievement would be bolstered by making learning powerful and memorable.

Gardner's theory proved flexible enough to respond to different intentions. Because MI is a construct about human intelligence, it does not mandate any prescriptive educational approach. Thus, the teachers and administrators at the six schools had the freedom to create educational practices that best fit their students' and their own needs.

Further, MI does not necessarily depend upon district or administrative approval. Because it can fit almost any instructional mode, teachers can use the theory as an instructional framework and then observe schoolwide change gather momentum when colleagues change their teaching practices. In fact, contrary to many restructuring efforts, four schools in our sample adopted MI not at the principal's request, but because teachers or other district personnel suggested it.

ONCE MI IS EMBRACED, THEN WHAT?

Each school we've studied had to decide how to explore and apply MI theory. Because these MI programs were created within five or six years of the publication of *Frames of Mind* in 1983, there were few models to emulate. To learn about MI, all schools sought out professional development. Such efforts consisted of holding study groups with one's colleagues at EXPO to attending institutes at Harvard by Mountlake Terrace High School teachers. Other options included inservice courses, school visits, conference attendance, and staff-created libraries. While professional development took numerous forms, so too did the program designs that emerged from such efforts.

Each of the six schools created MI programmatic features that are distinct from the offerings at other schools. For example, every year at Russell Elementary School, primary students write, produce, and perform an opera. EXPO offers Theaters of Learning to accommodate student choice and interest. Skyview Junior High has created the award-winning Breakout! project, where students tap their individual strengths to enhance their local communities. The Key Learning Community bases its total school program on MI outcomes, and Lincoln High School promotes Integrated Studies courses. Mountlake Terrace High School makes student graduation contingent upon the successful completion of a community-mentored, interdisciplinary project.

Though each school's expression of MI looks different from every other, closer scrutiny reveals striking similarities. It is as if while working in isolation, these six schools happened upon fundamental principles that are essential in any effective MI application. These principles are shown in Figure 5.1.

Figure 5.1

Fundamental Principles of Successful MI Programs

1. Teachers believe students are intellectually competent in multifaceted ways.

2. The school's mission, culture, and curriculum promote intellectual diversity.

3. Teachers become astute observers of students and adjust their instruction accordingly.

4. Student learning is active, hands-on, and multimodal.

5. Student strengths are used to improve academic weaknesses.

6. Students have opportunities to personalize their educational experiences while also acquiring basic skills.

7. Students develop autonomous learning skills through initiating and completing independent projects.

8. Students are mentored in their intelligence strengths by school or community experts.

9. Students study core disciplinary concepts in multi-age groupings or through interdisciplinary perspectives for in-depth understanding.

10. Students apply classroom learning in real-world contexts.

11. Assessment is as varied as instruction and includes performance-based measures, traditional tests, feedback from numerous sources, and active student self-assessment.

Even with the numerous national and local pressures placed on schools and what they must accomplish, the six studied in this book actually narrowed rather than expanded their focus. They identified a single purpose for their schools, which in turn provided the framework for their programs and pedagogy. Their mission was to nurture the intellectual development of all students.

Each school took the time to define its beliefs and missions. They grappled with significant questions such as: "What does our school stand for?" "What do we believe about our students and about teaching and learning?" "How do we ensure that our curriculum, structure, and teaching practices help us achieve our mission?" Intentionally designed school programs emerged from the answers to these questions. Teachers and administrators took hold of the curriculum at each site and shaped it to educate for human intelligence.

Although the teachers we interviewed adamantly maintain that all students can learn, they are equally adamant that all students do not learn alike.

Using MI as a guide, they refined their observation skills and recognized extensive differences among their students. They also acknowledged that no single approach works well for everyone, and that all students require choice and opportunities to personalize some of their educational experiences.

Consistently, at all six sites, much emphasis is placed upon the personal intelligences. This emphasis takes three forms. First, students are taught specific interpersonal and intrapersonal skills such as those featured in Russell's Character Education program or in Mountlake Terrace High School's self-directed application project. By making these skills explicit, students are better able to manage their social and academic behaviors.

Second, extensive curricular time is dedicated to student-selected interests. At Russell, students pursue intelligence majors, and at EXPO they select Theaters of Learning. At Key, middle school students choose yearlong pods and conduct service learning projects in intelligences of their choice. At Skyview Junior High School, students attend acceleration periods to develop their strengths or weaknesses. They also participate in Breakout!, where they contribute to their local communities through their individual intellectual strengths. At Mountlake Terrace and Lincoln High Schools, students conduct self-directed learning projects in most classes.

The personal intelligences are also emphasized through a strong sense of community at each school. For example, EXPO has "family groupings" of students who remain together for three years. Skyview features grade-level learning communities, and at Lincoln students pursue integrated studies programs that last one or more years. Further, teachers and administrators have reached out in new and significant ways to enlist parents in the education of their children, whether it be visiting homes when children are absent, hosting pizza parties or overnight events at the school, involving parents as intelligence mentors, or providing monthly Poet's Café events for parents and community members.

These six schools have expanded the traditional educational emphasis on linguistic and logical intelligences to include that of the personal and individual. They provide explicit instruction in inter- and intrapersonal skills, curricular dedication to student choice and self-direction, and the creation of an enhanced sense of community at the school and beyond. While most schools place linguistic and logical intelligences on an educational pedestal, at these six MI sites, the personal intelligences are equally esteemed.

IS MI GOOD FOR STUDENTS?

Educational innovations are usually considered effective if students perform well on a variety of tests. At the six MI schools, teachers shunned teaching to any test, and remained focused on teaching their curriculum. Nevertheless, their students are required to take state and national tests. The results are in, and they speak for themselves.

At inner-city Russell Elementary School, with 94 percent of its population on free and reduced lunch, student scores have doubled on Kentucky's state tests. Russell students outperform district and county peers, and with a percentage of 65 percent African American students, the discrepancy between black and white student scores has disappeared. At inner-city EXPO for Excellence Elementary School, where over 50 percent of the students are minority and 35 percent are limited-English-proficient, scores on the new Minnesota basic skills tests are among the highest in St. Paul. On the standardized Metropolitan Achievement Tests, EXPO students significantly outperform their peers locally and nationally.

Across the country, in a suburban, white middle-class community, students at Skyview Junior High Skyview likewise perform well on state and national tests. On the Comprehensive Test of Basic Skills, Skyview students exceed their state and national peers by 20 percentage points in reading, language arts, and math. On the new Washington state tests, Skyview students outperformed their district and state peers in reading, writing, listening, and math. Their achievement is all the more noteworthy because Skyview is the only junior high school out of five in its district that houses three levels of special-needs students: profound and medically fragile, self-contained, and those included in the regular classroom.

At the Key Learning Community in Indianapolis, students are not screened for enrollment but are admitted on a lottery system. Though curricular time is divided equitably among all intelligences without an undue emphasis upon logical and linguistic intelligences, Key middle school students exceed district goals on Indiana's new state tests. Further, with 50 percent minority students and nearly half on free and reduced lunch, Key 6th, 7th, and 8th graders score at grade level or above in all areas tested by the California Test of Basic Skills.

At Mountlake Terrace High School, state-administered test scores have risen from below to above district averages since adopting MI practices. On such tests, Terrace students outperform their statewide peers in English, math, and social studies. On Scholastic Aptitude Tests, Terrace students outperform state and national peers in math achievement.

At Lincoln High School in Stockton, California, standardized testing did not take place for a few years while state assessments were being developed. However, on the new Stanford Test of Academic Skills, Lincoln students score the highest in their county in nearly all subjects. On Scholastic Aptitude Tests, Lincoln students outscore district- and statewide peers. The school ranked second in its county for graduation rates, with over 97 percent of Lincoln seniors graduating from high school. Once they do, a remarkable 90 percent go on to attend college.

Although these achievement gains of MI programs are considered substantial by many, the teachers and administrators who work within the schools typically are nonplussed. They assert that such tests don't communicate the whole story of student accomplishment. State and national tests cannot reveal that students are engaged in personally relevant schoolwork, that they are developing a broad spectrum of intellectual competencies, that they can apply what they know, and that they can tell others what they are doing and why.

The scores risk placing standardized tests and not students at the center of public attention. They also obscure the educational mission that the teachers and administrators are pioneering: developing human intelligence. Nor do such scores reveal the enthusiasm of students for learning, their increased school attendance, or their enhanced self-perceptions. One thing the test scores do communicate, however, is that adopting MI does not mean ignoring the basics, but rather that MI can improve basic skill achievement and more.

AT MI SCHOOLS, THE ACHIEVEMENT GAP NARROWS

A remarkable finding we discovered at the MI schools is that disparity among white and minority student achievement has been reduced or eliminated. Attendance at four of the six sites—Russell Elementary, EXPO Elementary, Key Learning Community, and Lincoln High School—includes 50 percent or more minority students. Three of the schools—Russell, EXPO, and Key, have high percentages of students living in poverty. Typically, such populations would be considered at-risk, and many students would be placed in remedial and/or intervention programs.

By contrast, all students at the MI sites are immersed in challenging academic content and methodologies. Their teachers are philosophically opposed to remedial education and favor enrichment instead. The traditional model of education that requires students to work alone and listen to an instructor has been replaced with dynamic, multimodal learning, and flexible groupings of students and adult experts. Students are also intrinsically motivated by personally relevant curriculum and self-directed, investigative projects. Further, they understand that just as everyone is talented in one or more intelligences, most are challenged in one or more ways. This knowledge helps to eliminate the fear of failure and promotes the notion of working hard to overcome challenges. White and minority students at MI schools all acquire the basic skills, develop critical and creative thinking abilities, and experience the satisfaction of succeeding at demanding school tasks.

INSIGHTS GAINED ABOUT MI SCHOOLS

The fortuitous marriage of a cognitive theorist and teachers has caused dramatic changes in schools and the quality of education for thousands of children. Not intended originally for a school audience, MI has no formal policies and procedures for teachers to follow. Instead, the theory works in more subtle ways by freeing educators to work from their strengths and their knowledge of children.

Furthermore, the theory of multiple intelligences is singular in that seldom does a single concept alter the perceptions of students, instruction, and assessment. By believing that students have aptitude in several areas, educators are reconsidering their roles and responsibilities. In the past, research on effective schools has highlighted the necessity of holding high expectations for all students. MI specifies the kinds of expectations to attain. Strengths exist within everyone that all teachers can nurture and develop. Because of a positive and explicit belief in student intelligence, teaching practices change and, ultimately, so does student achievement.

Most of us become educators out of a desire to enhance the quality of life for children and youth. We work diligently to help students grow, develop, and learn. Throughout our years in teaching, we seek out new curriculum and methodologies, trying one approach after the other, hoping to discover those that are the most effective. Perhaps, the most surprising finding from our study of MI schools is that restructuring is not necessarily achieved through external programs, resources, facilities, or district or state mandates. Indeed, meaningful restructuring first takes place within the minds of teachers and their beliefs about the nature and possibilities of their students. From there, all else follows.

References

Bamburg, J. (1994). *Raising expectations to improve student learning.* Oak Brook, IL: North Central Regional Educational Laboratory, ED 378 290.

Barr, M. A., & Syverson, M. A. (1999). *Assessing literacy with the Learning Record: A handbook for teachers, grades 6–12.* Portsmouth, NH: Heinemann Books, Inc.

Brophy, J. E. (1983). Research on the self-fulfilling prophecy and teacher expectations. *Journal of Educational Psychology, 75*(5), 631–681.

Campbell, B. (1994). *The MI handbook: Lesson plans and more.* Stanwood, WA: Campbell & Associates, Inc.

Campbell, L. (1997, September). Variations on a theme: How teachers interpret MI Theory. *Educational Leadership, 55*(1), 14–19.

Campbell, L., & Campbell, B. (1995). *Multiple intelligences video series: Facilitator's guides.* Alexandria, VA: Association for Supervision and Curriculum Development.

Campbell, L., Campbell, B., & Dickinson, D. (1999, 1996). *Teaching and learning through multiple intelligences.* Needham Heights, MA: Allyn and Bacon.

Cooper, H. M., & Tom, D. Y. H. (1984, September). Teacher expectation research: A review with implications for classroom instruction. *The Elementary School Journal, 85*(1), 77–89.

Desombre, A. (1997, September). Telling parents about MI. *Classroom Leadership Online 1,* 1.

Gardner, H. (1983). *Frames of mind: The theory of multiple intelligences.* New York: Basic Books.

Gardner, H. (1991). *The unschooled mind: How children think and how schools should teach.* New York: Basic Books.

Good, T. L. (1987, July-August). Two decades of research on teacher expectations: Findings and future directions. *Journal of Teacher Education, 38*(4), 32–47.

Gould, S. J. (1981). *The mismeasure of man.* New York: W. W. Norton & Company.

Harvard Project Zero & Educational Testing Service. (1991). *Arts PROPEL: An introductory handbook.* Cambridge, MA: Harvard Graduate School of Education.

Kovalik, S. (1994). *Integrated thematic instruction: The model.* Kent, WA: Susan Kovalik & Associates.

Meisels, S. J. (1996, December/1997, January). Using work sampling in authentic assessments. *Educational Leadership, 54*(4), 60–65.

Piaget, J. (1952). *The origins of intelligence in children.* New York: International Press.

Quality Counts '98. (1998, January 8). The urban challenge: Public education in 50 states. *Education Week.*

Rist, R. C. (1970). Student social class and teacher expectations: The self-fulfilling prophecy in ghetto education. *Harvard Educational Review, 40*(3), 411–452.

Rosenthal, R., & Jacobson, L. (1968). *Pygmalion in the classroom: Teacher expectations and pupils' intellectual development.* New York: Holt, Rinehart & Winston, Inc.

The Seattle Times 1997-1998 School Guide. Seattle, WA: The Seattle Times Co.

Slavin, R. L. (1994). *Educational psychology: Theory and practice.* Needham Heights, MA: Allyn and Bacon.

Winfield, L. F. (1986). Teacher beliefs toward academically at risk students in inner urban schools. *The Urban Review, 18*(4), 253–268.

CONTACT INFORMATION AND VISITATION POLICIES FOR THE SIX MI SCHOOLS

EXPO for Excellence Elementary Magnet School
540 Warwick
St. Paul, MN 55116
Contact person: Principal Paul Osterlund
E-mail: paul.osterlund@spps.org
Phone: 651-290-8384
Website: http://www.expo1.stpaul.k12.mn.us/
Visitation policy: Flexible. Call to schedule.

The Key Learning Community
725 N. New Jersey St.
Indianapolis, IN 46202
Phone: 317-226-4992
Contact person: Myra Duff, School Liaison
Website: http://www.ips.k12.in.us/mskey/
Visitation policy: Thursdays only. Contact Myra Duff to schedule appointment.

Lincoln High School
Lincoln Unified School District
6844 Alexandria Pl.
Stockton, CA 95207
Phone: 209-953-8921
Contact persons: Principal Norrie Bean
                          Principal Louise King
Website: http://intergate.lincolnusd.k12.ca.us/lhs/
Visitation policy: Flexible. Call to schedule.

M.I.A.M.I. (Magnet for the Integrated Arts Through the Multiple Intelligences) at Russell Elementary School
201 W. Fifth St.
Lexington, KY 40508
Contact person: Principal Edwina Smith
Phone: 606-381-3576
E-mail: esmith@fayette.k12.ky.us
Visitation policy: Visitor do's and don'ts (posted outside each classroom) state: Come in and find an inconspicuous place to stand. Don't take photos or videos. Expect to have long conversations with others.

Mountlake Terrace High School
21801 44th Ave. W.
Mountlake Terrace, WA 98043-3598
Phone: 425-670-7776
Contact person: Principal Mark Baker
Contact teachers: Dan Wilson, Biology
                            Eeva Reeder, Math
                            Kate Cleaval, Special Education
                            Jay Kirk, Language Arts
Website: http://www.edmonds.wednet.edu/mths/
Visitation policy: Call to schedule.

Skyview Junior High School
21404 35th Ave. SE
Bothell, WA 98021-7869
Office phone: 425-489-6040
Contact person: Principal Holly Call
Principal's phone: 425-402-5150
Website: http://www.norshore.wednet.edu
E-mail: hcall@nsd.org
Visitation policy: Once monthly. Call to schedule.

INDEX

Note: An *f* after a page number indicates a figure on that page.

ABOUT THE AUTHORS

Linda Campbell is Professor of Education and Director of the Center for Community and Professional Learning at Antioch University Seattle. **Bruce Campbell** is a Teacher and Staff Development Specialist for the Marysville School District in Washington State. The Campbells coauthored the best-seller *Teaching and Learning Through Multiple Intelligences,* published by Allyn and Bacon; the *Facilitator's Guides* for ASCD's *Multiple Intelligences Video Series;* and numerous articles, chapters, and books on improving student learning. They may be contacted at 17410 Marine Dr., Stanwood, WA 98292. Fax: 360-652-9503. E-mail (Linda Campbell): lindacam@premier1.net. E-mail (Bruce Campbell): bc122@yahoo.com.

RELATED ASCD RESOURCES: MULTIPLE INTELLIGENCES

Audiotapes

Authentic Assessment Using the Multiple Intelligences

How Multiple Intelligences and Learning Style Fit: The Research and Practical Applications

Multiple Assessments for Multiple Intelligences by Beth Swartz

Multiple Intelligences—Putting a Theory into Practice by Helen Flamm, Connie Canter, Ernest Flamm, and Carolyn Wheeler

Multiple Intelligences Team Building and Class Building

On Multiple Intelligences and Education by Howard Gardner

Teaching for Understanding Through Multiple Intelligences by Geni Boyer

Teaching Thinking to Multiple Intelligences and Diverse Student Populations by Richard Strong

CD-ROMs

Exploring Our Multiple Intelligences

Online Courses

Multiple Intelligences Professional Development course

Print Products

ASCD Topic Pack—*Multiple Intelligences*

Becoming a Multiple Intelligences School by Thomas R. Hoerr

Multiple Intelligences in the Classroom by Thomas Armstrong

Videotapes

The Multiple Intelligences Series by Bruce and Linda Campbell

For more information about these resources, visit us on the World Wide Web (**http://www.ascd.org**), send an e-mail message to member@ascd.org, call the ASCD Service Center (1-800-933-ASCD or 703-578-9600, then press 2), send a fax to 703-575-5400, or write to Information Services, ASCD, 1703 N. Beauregard St., Alexandria, VA 22311-1714 USA.